MW00585763

BOOK I OF THE ORTHODOX LITURGY SERIES

The Anointing of the Sick

Paul Meyendorff

ST VLADIMIR'S SEMINARY PRESS
CRESTWOOD, NEW YORK
2009

Library of Congress Cataloging-in-Publication Data

Meyendorff, Paul.
  The anointing of the sick / Paul Meyendorff.
    p. cm. — (The Orthodox liturgy series ; bk. 1)
  Includes bibliographical references.
  ISBN 978-0-88141-187-4
    1. Orthodox Eastern Church.   2. Unction.   3. Church work with the
  sick—Orthodox Eastern Church.   4. Unction—Liturgy—Texts.   I. Title.

BX323.M49 2009
264'.019087—dc22

                                                        2009003136

© 2009 BY PAUL MEYENDORFF

ST VLADIMIR'S SEMINARY PRESS
575 Scarsdale Rd, Crestwood, NY 10707
1-800-204-2665
www.svspress.com

All rights reserved. No part of this book may be reproduced or
transmitted in any form or by any means, electronic or mechanical,
including photocopying, recording, or by any information storage
and retrieval system, except as may be expressly permitted by the
1976 Copyright Act, or in writing from the publisher.

ISBN 978-0-88141-187-4

PRINTED IN THE UNITED STATES OF AMERICA

For my wife, Peggy

CONTENTS

Introduction

Healing is too important to be left solely to the medical profession. Yet that is exactly what our modern society has done. The sick are herded into large hospitals, hooked up to an ever-increasing array of machines, and pumped full of wonder drugs. Using modern technology, physicians are now able to prolong "life" almost indefinitely. Many once-deadly diseases have been eliminated or become curable. Physical pain can be controlled, if not totally eliminated. A vast, impersonal medical bureaucracy, controlled by doctors, governments, and insurance companies, has arisen, reaching deep into the life (and pockets) of every individual.

Yet this remarkable medical progress comes with a price. Sickness and dying have become the responsibility of a medical establishment which treats humans merely as mechanisms that have broken down and need repair (or are beyond repair). The sick are removed from their homes, separated from their families, jobs, churches—from society. Their bodies are invaded, poked, and probed as physicians and other health professionals perform their duties. But who cares for their emotional and spiritual well-being? In recent years, hospitals have hired increasing numbers of social workers and chaplains, but these are very much junior partners in the medical enterprise, often barely tolerated by the "professionals." Doctors remain very much the "high priests" of the medical system we have created for ourselves.

As a society, we have chosen to leave healing to the medical profession. Doctors and hospitals have all the knowledge and technology, and we are perfectly happy to leave everything in their hands. Our consciences are clear when we provide our loved ones—our parents, our spouses, our children—with the best medical care money can buy.

Hospitals, nursing homes, long-term care facilities not only provide medical care, but also insulate the rest of us from having to come face-to-face with pain, suffering, death, and our own mortality. "Leave it to the professionals," we say, "that's their job." Rationalizing in this way, we keep sickness out of sight and out of mind; we postpone facing the reality of sickness and death as long as possible, until we must each face it on our own, unprepared as we are.

As a result, while we may be very good at addressing the physical aspects of sickness, we altogether neglect its spiritual side. Yet the spiritual suffering which accompanies physical illness can often be far worse than any physical pain. Separation from family and church, guilt, the anxiety caused by facing one's mortality, the loss of control over one's life—all these can be sources of agonizing pain. Writing in the nineteenth century, Leo Tolstoy described the agonizing suffering endured by Ivan Ilich, a well-to-do provincial judge:

> The doctor said that his physical suffering was terrible, and that was true; but more terrible than his physical suffering was his spiritual suffering, and in this lay his chief agony . . .
>
> He lay down on his back and began to pass his life in review in an entirely new fashion . . . He saw himself, all that he had been living by, and saw clearly all that was not right, that it was all a terrible, huge deception, which concealed

both life and death. This consciousness increased, multiplied tenfold his physical sufferings.[1]

This pain the medical doctors could not cure. True healing, which is both physical and spiritual, can be given only by Christ, who is the "Physician of our souls and bodies."

This healing ministry of Christ is a primary task of the Church, which is the presence of Christ in this sick and fallen world. We are Christ's presence in the world, and we, as the Church, are charged with bringing healing to those around us. At the Last Judgment, we shall have to answer whether we "fed the poor, welcomed the stranger, clothed the naked, visited the sick . . ." (Matt 25.31–46). Our contemporary church life is sorely lacking in this regard. Few parishes encourage their members to engage in this ministry, which is often simply forgotten or left up to the priest alone. Few communities make full and appropriate use of the sacrament of healing, the anointing of the sick. We do not even make this ministry of healing available to our own parishioners, or to members of our own families, who are all too often left to suffer and die alone, in hospitals and nursing homes. For this we shall be held accountable.

In this work, we shall look briefly at the healing ministry of the Church as it is expressed in Scripture and tradition. We shall focus on the sacrament of anointing of the sick, with the hope that this rite can once more assume its prominent role in ecclesial life. In this hope, a new translation of the rite is appended, together with an abbreviated version more suitable in certain circumstances.

---

[1]Leo Tolstoy, *The Death of Ivan Ilich,* The Collected Works 9, Leo Wiener, trans. (New York: Willey Book Company, 1904), 75–6.

Healing is far too important to be left to the medical professions alone.

Paul Meyendorff
St Vladimir's Orthodox Theological Seminary
Pentecost 2008

CHAPTER 1

The Healing Ministry of the Church

H ealing lies at the very center of the Church's ministry. Even a quick review of Scripture and early Christian writings makes this clear, and there is no rite or sacrament which does not contain some reference to healing. We have but to listen to the Sunday gospel readings or hear the words of liturgical prayers to realize just how frequently the theme recurs. Thus the specific rite of healing, the "Anointing of the Sick," is but one aspect of this ministry and needs to be examined in its broader context.

Jesus the Healer

When John the Baptist sent his disciples to the Lord to ask if he was the Messiah, Jesus answered them:

> The blind receive their sight and the lame walk, lepers are cleansed and the deaf hear, and the dead are raised up, and the poor have good news preached to them. (Matt 11.5; see Isa 35.5–6)

Jesus comes to proclaim the inauguration of the kingdom, and his miracles are signs that the kingdom is at hand. The miracles both portray what the kingdom is like and initiate it. Jesus' healing ministry is therefore an integral part of his teaching, in which his words and his actions form one consistent whole.

> And Jesus went about all the cities and villages, teaching in their synagogues and preaching the gospel of the kingdom, and healing every disease and every infirmity. (Matt 9.35)

Jesus' purpose in healing those who flocked to him is not to instill awe and fear, or even to draw attention to himself. He instructs the leper to tell no one but the priest what has happened.[1] When crowds come to him expecting more miracles, he escapes across the Sea of Galilee.[2] When he heals the paralytic at the Pool of Bethesda, crowds gather and again he departs.[3] Rather, Jesus' purpose is to manifest God's presence, to inaugurate his kingdom.

The healings of Jesus must be seen within the context of his entire ministry. Even in the New Testament accounts, two elements are characteristically connected to the healing of sickness— faith and repentance.

Faith is presented in the gospels as either preceding or following healing.

> And behold, a woman who had suffered from a hemorrhage for twelve years came up behind him and touched the fringe of his garment; for she said to herself, "If I only touch his garment, I shall be made well." Jesus turned, and seeing her he

[1]Matt 8.4; see also 9.30.
[2]Matt 8.18.
[3]John 5.13.

said, "Take heart, daughter, your faith has made you well."
(Matt 9.20–22)

This faith is exhibited in the gospels not only by Jews, but also by
Gentiles, as is evident in the case of the Roman centurion who
asks Jesus to heal his paralyzed servant. "Not even in Israel have
I found such faith," Jesus answers before granting his request.[4]
The Son of God comes to save all humanity. Sometimes, also,
faith follows healing, as in the case of the man born blind.[5]

Closely linked to the power to heal is the power to forgive sins.
Jesus begins by forgiving the sins of the paralytic, and only then
performs the healing.[6] This provokes the ire of the scribes and
Pharisees. Experts in Jewish law, they know that only God can
forgive sins; how can the man Jesus be so presumptuous as to
assume this divine prerogative? In this account, we see clearly that
remission of sins takes precedence over the healing of disease. We
see that Jesus' healing ministry addresses the entire person. We
learn that physical illness is but a symptom of the sickness that
pervades the whole world, which has its source in sin (though not
necessarily the individual sin of the sick person). In this case, Jesus
removes the source of the illness before he cures the symptoms.

This close connection between sin and sickness, we shall see,
lies at the very heart of the Church's healing ministry. Physical
healing is not an end in itself, but must always be seen in the context of Jesus' ministry, which is to reconcile the world with God.
He came to inaugurate the kingdom, which will be consummated
only when he returns in glory at the second coming. Indeed, those

[4]Matt 8.5–13; Luke 7.1–10; John 4.46–53; see also the story of the
Syrophoenician woman in Mark 7.24–30, or that of the Canaanite woman
in Matt 14.21–29.
[5]John 9.
[6]Matt 9.2–8; Mark 2.1–12; Luke 5.17–26.

Jesus healed or raised from the dead all got sick again and died. The healings, therefore, only foreshadow what is yet to come.

In their immediate context, the healings of Jesus often aim to reintegrate the sick person into the community of faith. This is evident particularly in the very first cure Jesus performs, the healing of the leper.[7] After the man is well, the Lord instructs him:

> See that you say nothing to anyone; but go, show yourself to the priest, and offer for your cleansing what Moses commanded, for a proof to the people. (Mark 1.44)

Thus cleansed, the man is now able to resume his place in the synagogue or the Temple, from which he had been excluded because of his illness. By performing this healing, therefore, the Lord restores the proper relationship between God and the creature, a relationship which sin, sickness, and death have mutilated.

It would be inaccurate, however, to see these healings as mere object lessons. While all the evangelists use the miracle stories to explain who Jesus was—Son of God, Messiah, the Promised One, who has power over all creation—the healings also show him to be both loving and compassionate. He weeps at the tomb of his friend Lazarus. He heals on the Sabbath, showing that mercy is more important than strict observance of the law. He cares particularly for the poor and the outcast, for those who have no one to help them.

The Healing Ministry in the Apostolic Church

Already during his earthly ministry, our Lord appoints his disciples to carry out the very same task:

[7]Mark 1.40–44; Matt 8.2–4; Luke 5.12–16.

And he called to him the twelve, and began to send them out two by two, and gave them authority over the unclean spirits. . . . So they went out and preached that men should repent. And they cast out many demons, and anointed with oil many that were sick and healed them. (Mark 6.7–12; see also Matt 10.1–15; Luke 9.1–6)

When the seventy return from their mission, they report with joy to their Master: "Lord, even the demons are subject to us in your name!"[8] Thus, healing is an integral part of the ministry of the apostles. Soon after Pentecost, Peter heals the man born lame, and the man immediately enters the temple with Peter and John, where they preach about Jesus Christ to the Jews.[9] The apostles continue to perform healings as signs of the kingdom,[10] but we find no emphasis on miraculous cures in the rest of the New Testament corpus.

We find instead a focus on the life of the community, on the Church as the body of Christ, on the responsibility of each member of the body to work for the upbuilding of the Church, on unity and mutual responsibility. In the primitive community of Jerusalem, Christians held everything in common, "and they sold their possessions and goods and distributed them to all, as any had need."[11] While this radically communal form of living does not seem to have extended beyond Jerusalem, the New Testament writings stress the unity of the Church, as St Paul summarizes in his First Epistle to the Corinthians:

[8]Luke 10.17.
[9]Acts 3–4.
[10]See Acts 9.32–43.
[11]Acts 2.44–45.

But God has so composed the body, giving the greater honor
to the inferior part, that there may be no discord in the body,
but that the members may have the same care for one another.
If one member suffers, all suffer together; if one member is
honored, all rejoice together. Now you are the body of Christ
and individually members of it. (1 Cor 12.24–27)

St Paul urges his readers to care for one another. He preaches the
gospel of love.[12] He takes up collections for the church in
Jerusalem.[13] All must use their gifts and talents for the upbuilding of the Church, the body of Christ. He criticizes the Corinthians precisely for failing to be united:

When you assemble as a church, I hear that there are divisions
among you. . . . When you meet together, it is not the Lord's
Supper that you eat. For in eating, each one goes ahead with
his own meal. (1 Cor 11.18–21)

Within this closely-knit community, all are expected to care
for one another, to love one another. This is at the very basis of
the ethical teachings of Christ. We must love our neighbor as ourselves.[14] We shall be judged on whether we feed the hungry, give
drink to the thirsty, visit the sick and the prisoners.[15] When a
member falls into sin, the community is charged with healing the
wound, because the whole community is wounded.[16] Those in
serious sin are to be cast out, so that they may be healed.[17] As

[12]1 Cor 13.
[13]1 Cor 16.1–4.
[14]Matt 22.39; Mark 12.31; Luke 10.27.
[15]Parable of the Last Judgment: Matt 25.31–46.
[16]Matt 18.15–18; see also 1 Cor 12.26.
[17]1 Cor 5.

Christ laid down his life for us, so all Christians are called to live for the other, even to the point of giving up their own lives.[18]

The very purpose of the Church is to heal us, to restore the rift between God and humanity which is caused by our sin and leads to death. This is achieved precisely when we are united to one another and to God in the body of Christ, which is the Church. In his high-priestly prayer, our Lord prays for all his followers,

> That they may all be one; even as you, Father, are in me, and I in you, that they also may be in us, so that the world may believe that you have sent me. The glory which you have given me I have given to them, that they may be one even as we are one, I in them and you in me, that they may become perfectly one, so that the world may know that you have sent me and have loved them even as you have loved me. (John 17.21–23)

Jesus Christ is here asking for nothing less than the healing of the whole world, all humanity, all creation. This is achieved when we come to know Christ, when we become one with him and with one another. Everything that the Church does, all its sacramental and liturgical life, all its teaching, is directed at restoring the proper relationship between God and creation, which has been corrupted through our sinfulness. This is the real meaning of Christian healing, and it involves the whole person, body, soul, and spirit. The locus of this healing ministry is the Church's sacraments, and particularly its rites of initiation: baptism/chrismation and the eucharist.

---

[18]John 15.13.

Baptism: Sacrament of Healing

In baptism, Christian converts abandon their old life, in which they were under the sway of sin and death, and enter into a new life, where sin and death have been defeated. Nowhere is this more clearly expressed than in St Paul's letter to the Romans:

> Do you not know that all of us who have been baptized into Christ were baptized into his death? We were buried therefore with him by baptism into death, so that as Christ was raised from the dead by the glory of the Father, we too might walk in newness of life. . . .
>
> For if we have been united with him in a death like his, we shall certainly be united with him in a resurrection like his. We know that our old self was crucified with him so that the sinful body might be destroyed, and that we might no longer be enslaved to sin. For he who has died is freed from sin. But if we have died with Christ, we believe that we shall also live with him. For we know that Christ being raised from the dead will never die again; death no longer has dominion over him. The death he died he died to sin, once for all, but the life he lives he lives to God. So you also must consider yourselves dead to sin and alive to God in Christ Jesus. (Rom 6.3–11)[19]

In baptism, we enter into a new relationship with God, with Christ, in which sin, sickness, and death no longer dominate. We become children of God, heirs of the kingdom, members of Christ's body, the Church. This new relationship is to endure for ever, and neither sickness nor death can destroy it. It is a new form of human existence. Our head is no longer the "old Adam," who brought sin, sickness, and death into the world, but Christ, the

[19]Text read at the service of baptism.

"new Adam," who "destroys death by death" and gives us eternal life.

Baptism, therefore, is the sacrament of healing par excellence, a healing aimed at the whole person, body, soul, and spirit. This is clearly expressed in the central prayer of the baptismal rite, the blessing of water, at the invocation of the Holy Spirit:

> Therefore O loving King, come now and sanctify this water by the indwelling of your Holy Spirit, and grant to it the grace of redemption, the blessing of Jordan; make it the fountain of incorruption, the gift of sanctification, the remission of sins, the remedy of infirmities. . . .

> But do you, O Master of all, show this water to be the water of redemption, the water of sanctification, the purification of flesh and spirit, the loosing of bonds, the remission of sins, the illumination of the soul, the washing of regeneration, the renewal of the spirit, the gift of adoption to sonship, the garment of incorruption, the fountain of life . . .

Baptism therefore introduces us into a new life, in communion with God and with one another. Our sins are forgiven; we are born anew as members of the Church, which is Christ's body. In this new life, sickness and death no longer have the same power over us, for they have been defeated. Sickness and death continue to exist, but they now mark not the end of our existence, but a transition to eternal life, a passage into the kingdom. Just as Christ himself died and rose again, so we too shall die and rise. In Christ, our ultimate defeat is transformed into victory!

The whole baptismal process is characterized by this healing process. It begins with the catechumenate, which was once spread over a period of several years. The exorcisms, once recited daily or weekly over a period of several years, but now recited just before baptism, contain numerous references to healing, not only spiritual, but also physical. The blessing prayer over the oil of the catechumens, used for pre-baptismal anointing, is an ancient prayer of healing and asks for the "renewing of soul and body." The prayer read just prior to chrismation contains a petition for deliverance from the workings of the devil, which certainly includes sickness and death. The epistle reading, Romans 6.3–11, stresses the victory over death effected by baptism, and thus places healing in an entirely new perspective.

After baptism, we experience our personal Pentecost as hands are laid upon us and we receive anointing with chrism, the seal of the gift of the Holy Spirit. The destructive spirit within us has been expelled, drowned in the waters of baptism, in the colorful image of St Cyril of Jerusalem.[20] Now, the Holy Spirit is invited to enter and abide in the newly baptized. We become the temple of the Holy Spirit, a new creation. We are incorporated into the Church, the body of Christ, enlivened by the Spirit. We become "christs" (the Greek word, *christos*, means "anointed"). And we, the Church, become the presence of Christ in the world, charged with bringing the same healing message of Christ to the whole world.

> Go therefore and make disciples of all nations, baptizing them in the name of the Father and of the Son and of the Holy Spirit, teaching them to observe all that I have commanded you; and lo, I am with you always, to the close of the age. (Matt 28.19–20)

Baptism, therefore, is the paradigmatic healing sacrament. Fallen humanity is recreated; our sins are forgiven; the image of God in us is restored; real, intimate communion with God,

[20]Cyril of Jerusalem, *Mystagogical Catechesis* I, 3, in *Lectures on the Christian Sacraments* (Crestwood, NY: SVS Press, 1986), 54.

destroyed because of sin, is again made possible. The sickness and death which once ruled our lives are defeated, in the sense that they, just like the cross, become a means of victory and a passage into the kingdom. The brokenness of our human existence is abolished as we are incorporated into the Church, the body of Christ, through which we are saved. We are no longer left to live out our lives alone, to suffer and die a meaningless death. Rather, in the Church, our suffering and death become a means to victory, following in the footsteps of Christ, his death on the cross and his resurrection. Through baptism, we are healed, and we are charged to bring this healing ministry to the world around us, to our family, to our neighbor, to all whom we encounter.

Eucharist: Medicine of Immortality

While baptism and chrismation are the means by which we become members of the Church, the body of Christ, the eucharist is the means by which this membership is realized and lived out on an ongoing basis. In fact, all the sacraments of the Church, as well as the daily and weekly cycles of prayer, have the eucharist as their goal. We are the Church precisely when we gather together, Sunday after Sunday, to celebrate the mystery of Christ's incarnation, death, and resurrection on our behalf. In the eucharist, we not only remember these events, but we become partakers of Christ, sharing in his divine nature. It is precisely in the eucharist that the famous fourth-century dictum of St Athanasius becomes actual: "God became man, so that man might become god."[21] This is the basis for the Orthodox teaching about divinization, or theosis.

---

[21]Athanasius, *On the Incarnation*, 54.3; cf. Athanasius, *On the Incarnation* (PPS 3; Crestwood, NY: SVS Press, 1977), 93.

Humanity is created to be in communion with God, and the eucharist is the realization of this communion. And true healing, as we have already seen, is precisely the restoration of communion with God, the restoration of the proper relationship between God and humanity. Every time we receive communion, we receive this grace of healing. As with baptism, this healing affects the entire person, with salvation, our entrance into the kingdom, as its ultimate goal.

The eucharistic liturgy contains as well numerous references to healing of both body and soul. Several of the litanies include a petition for the sick and the suffering, and for their salvation, as do the intercessions in the anaphoras of both St John Chrysostom and St Basil the Great. Characteristic is the following excerpt from the anaphoral intercessions of the Liturgy of St Basil:

> Remember, O Lord, the people here present and also those who are absent for honorable reasons. Have mercy on them and on us according to the multitude of your mercies. Fill their treasuries with every good thing; preserve their marriages in peace and harmony; raise the infants; guide the young; support the aged; encourage the fainthearted; reunite the separated; lead back those who are in error and join them to your holy, catholic, and apostolic Church; free those who are held captive by unclean spirits; sail with those who sail; travel with those who travel by land and by air; defend the widows; protect the orphans; free the captives; heal the sick. . . . For you, O Lord, are the Helper of the helpless, the Hope of the hopeless, the Savior of the bestormed, the Haven of the voyager, the Physician of the sick.

Just before communion, each of us prays that "the communion of your holy mysteries be neither to my judgment, nor to my condemnation, O Lord, but to the healing of soul and body." In the prayer of the litany of thanksgiving after communion from the Liturgy of St Basil (which was, until the tenth century, the regular Sunday liturgy, though it is now used mostly during Great Lent), we pray:

> We thank you, O Lord, for the participation in your holy, most-pure, immortal and heavenly mysteries, which you have granted us for the good and sanctification and healing of our souls and bodies.

In the eucharist, therefore, we find the continuation of Christ's healing ministry. When every Sunday we gather together in his name, Christ is present among us. He is present in the bread and wine, which become his body and blood. He is present in his word, which is read and proclaimed. He is present in us, because we, the Church, are the body of Christ. In this way we are all fed, restored, and healed; we recover our true identity as bearers of the image and likeness of God, in communion with our Creator; our citizenship in God's kingdom is affirmed. This, we have seen, is the true aim of all Christian healing.

The Life in Christ

While baptism and the eucharist certainly have a privileged role in the life of the Church, they are complemented by a rich liturgical tradition consisting of sacraments and other rites, such as marriage, penance, ordination, and various blessings, as well as the daily, weekly, and annual cycles of prayer. This liturgical life is further enriched by the practice of personal prayer, fasting, charitable work, and by countless examples of sanctity down to our own century, as well as by numerous miraculous occurrences of all sorts, often including healings which modern medicine cannot explain.

Every sacramental rite contains an element of healing. In the rite of marriage, for example, the earthly union, celebrated in the rite of betrothal, is transformed by the crowning into a mystery of the kingdom. Thus Christian marriage becomes eternal; and as long as both parties remain faithful and united to one another and to God, not even sickness and death can break the bond which God has forged. In the sacrament of ordination, the presiding bishop lays his hand on the candidate's head and prays:

> Your grace divine, *which always heals that which is infirm*, and completes that which is wanting, elevates, through the laying on of hands, the most devout [sub-deacon, deacon, priest] to be a [deacon, priest, bishop]. Therefore let us pray for him, that the grace of the all-holy Spirit may come upon him.

The sacrament of penance has as its main goal healing from sin, reconciliation with the Church, and restoration into communion. It is the continuation of the healing power of baptism, a restoration into the life of grace from which we fall because of our sins. The following prayer, recited by the priest over the head of the penitent at the conclusion of the rite, neatly summarizes this:

> O Lord God of the salvation of your servants, gracious, bountiful, and longsuffering, you repent concerning our evil deeds and desire not the death of a sinner, but that he(she) should turn from his(her) wickedness and live: show your mercy now upon your servant (name), and grant him(her) an image of repentance, forgiveness of sins, and deliverance, pardoning all his(her) transgressions, whether voluntary or involuntary.

Reconcile and unite him(her) to your holy Church, through Jesus Christ our Lord, with whom to you are due dominion and majesty, now and ever, and to the ages of ages. Amen.

Prayers for the blessing of various objects usually contain references to healing. Typical is the ending of the prayer for blessing the *artos*, a paschal bread, at the conclusion of the paschal liturgy:

Grant that we who offer this and those who shall kiss it and shall taste of it, may become partakers of your heavenly blessing. And by your might cast out every sickness and infirmity among us, granting health to all, for you are the fount of blessing and the bestower of health, and to you we give the glory, to the Father . . . the Son . . . and the Spirit.

The daily cycle of prayer is similarly replete with references to physical and spiritual illness, from which we ask to be released. The six psalms of matins, chanted by a reader in a darkened church, are a plea for God's mercy:

O Lord, rebuke me not in your anger, nor chasten me in your wrath! For your arrows have sunk into me, and your hand has come down on me. There is no soundness in my flesh because of your indignation; there is no health in my bones because of my sin. For my iniquities have gone over my head; they weigh like a burden too heavy for me. My wounds grow foul and fester because of my foolishness, I am utterly bowed down and prostrate; all the day I go about mourning. For my loins are filled with burning, and there is no soundness in my flesh. . . .

Do not forsake me, O Lord! O my God, be not far from me! Make haste to help me, O Lord, my salvation! (Ps 38[37].1–7, 21–22)

Overwhelmed by sin, sickness, and suffering, we can only turn to God and plead for mercy. Our entreaties are answered, for soon the church is flooded with light, and in triumph we sing, "God is the Lord and has revealed himself to us."[22] At vespers, we see the same themes reiterated: "Out of the depths I cry to you, O Lord! Lord, hear my voice! Let your ears be attentive to the voice of my supplications!"[23] Again we receive our answer as the church is illuminated and the choir sings the ancient evening hymn, "O Gladsome Light." For God, and God alone, is the true source of light, joy, salvation, and healing. In this way, each day we are given the opportunity to experience both our alienation from God, which is the result of our sin, and also salvation and healing, which come as free gifts from God.

The weekly and annual cycles of feasts and fasts similarly focus on the redemption offered us through the incarnation, death, and resurrection of Christ. Every Sunday the Church gathers to remember and celebrate the resurrection, to experience already in this world the life of the kingdom. This is why so many of the Sunday gospel readings are either parables of the kingdom or accounts of miraculous healings—these are already signs of the kingdom's presence. The center of the church year is the triumphant celebration of Pascha, which marks the victory of Christ over death, and therefore our own release from slavery to sin, sickness, and death. For forty days, we never cease to sing the paschal troparion:

> Christ is risen from the dead, trampling down death by death, and upon those in the tombs bestowing life!

[22]Ps 118[117].27.
[23]Ps 130[129].1–2.

Pascha, the victory over death, anchors the Church's liturgy of time. We are always either celebrating this victory—as we do in the fifty-day period from Pascha to Pentecost, as well as in feasts such as the Dormition and the memorials of saints—or preparing to do so by commemorating all the events leading up to it, beginning with the Annunciation.

Through the liturgy of time, the daily, weekly, and annual cycles of prayer, we are incorporated into salvation history. We live out our lives not as separate individuals, but as members of the body of Christ, into which we are incorporated through baptism, chrismation, and the eucharist. In this way we transcend the brokenness, the isolation, the sickness of our fallen world. While sickness, suffering, and death certainly remain a part of our lives, their power over us is broken, because they lead not to annihilation, but to eternal life in the kingdom.

In addition to having a rich tradition of common, liturgical prayer, the Church has always encouraged her members to pray. Jesus prayed often, and he taught his disciples to pray. Just as Jews prayed several times a day, so the early Christians developed a tradition of praying at least three times a day. According to the *Didache*, the earliest extant "Church Order," dating to the early second century, Christians must recite the Lord's Prayer three times a day. In fact, it is precisely this discipline of private prayer which subsequently develops into the daily cycle of liturgical prayer. Thus the private prayer of every individual Christian is but an extension of the prayer of the whole Church. Just as the Church gathers to pray for herself, for her members, and for the whole world, so each Christian is called to do the same. We pray for ourselves, for our families, for our neighbors, for the world around us; we pray for their individual and collective healing and salvation.

Constant, persistent prayer has always been the hallmark of Christianity. "Pray without ceasing," St Paul tells the Thessalonians.[24] "The prayer of a righteous man has great power in its effects," St James tells the Church.[25] We are taught to be persistent, never to stop praying and interceding for one another. Like the Canaanite woman, we learn to keep asking, not out of pride, but in humility.[26] And, as with this Canaanite woman, our prayers for healing are often answered, though not always at a time or in a way that we expect.

In short, every aspect of the ongoing life of the Church and her members involves an element of healing. The liturgical life, expressed in the sacraments, in the daily, weekly, and annual cycles of prayer, as well as the individual prayers of each Christian—all these are integral parts of the Church's healing ministry in all its aspects. This is because healing is at the very center of the Church's mission of preaching the gospel. And the paradigmatic healing sacrament is baptism, where humanity's wounds are healed. Christians are called to carry on this ministry by baptizing all nations, thus making this healing available to all.

[24] I Thess 5.17.
[25] Jas 5.16.
[26] Matt 15.22–28.

CHAPTER 2

A Brief History of the Rite of Anointing the Sick

Is any among you suffering? Let him pray. Is any cheerful? Let him sing praise. Is any among you sick? Let him call for the elders of the church, and let them pray over him, anointing him with oil in the name of the Lord; and the prayer of faith will save the sick man, and the Lord will raise him up; and if he has committed sins, he will be forgiven. Therefore confess your sins to one another, and pray for one another, that you may be healed. (Jas 5.13–16)

The Early Church

Just as the apostles sent out by Jesus healed the sick, so too this ministry was continued in the early Church, as the above passage from the Epistle of James demonstrates. Just as the Church cared for widows and orphans, took collections for the poor, so it ministered to her ill members. While the Church's primary mission always focused on spreading the gospel of Christ, love and care for the neighbor were always essential aspects of that mission. Besides the scriptural passages mentioned in the previous chapter, however, we have precious little information about just how this ministry was actually carried out in the primitive Church. We have to content ourselves with occasional references and a few liturgical texts.

In the ancient world, long before the modern hospital and the sophisticated technology of modern medicine, anointing with oil was commonly practiced by pagans and Jews alike. Olive oil, abundant in the Mediterranean world, was the "aspirin" of the age. Philo, the first-century Jewish writer, notes that Syrians, Babylonians, Indians, and Scythians all prepared special ointments using oil and other ingredients.[1] It was commonly used among the Romans also. Thus the Christian practice of using oil was nothing new, simply the Christianization of elements from the cultures in which they lived. This should hardly surprise us, since all the sacraments take as their starting point elements and actions from daily life—washing, eating, drinking, the laying on of hands. There is nothing uniquely Christian about any of these. What makes them Christian is their integration with prayer and thanksgiving, their inclusion in the life of the Church and of each of her members.

In the post-apostolic Church, the earliest evidence for healing oil is found in the *Apostolic Tradition* of Hippolytus, an early church order, dating possibly to the early third century, which strongly influenced eastern practice.[2] Here, oil for the sick is blessed at the eucharistic liturgy, immediately after the consecration of the bread and wine:

[1]Philo, *De somniis* II.
[2]The dating, authorship, and provenance of the *Apostolic Tradition* are all uncertain and continue to be debated by scholars. See, for example, the presentation on these matters by Alistair Stewart-Sykes in Hippolytus, *On the Apostolic Tradition* (Crestwood, NY: SVS Press, 2001), 11–50. For the sake of simplicity, we continue to refer to this work as "Hippolytus."

> If someone offers oil, he [the bishop] gives thanks in the same way as he has given thanks over the bread and the wine—not in the use of the same words, but rather in the same spirit—saying: "O God, as you make this oil holy, bestow your holiness upon those who are anointed with it. This is the oil with which you have anointed kings, priests, and prophets; grant that it may bring comfort to those who taste it, and health to those who use it."[3]

This passage, adapted to fit new contexts, is repeated in later church orders that incorporate Hippolytus' text, including, for example, the late fourth-century *Apostolic Constitutions*.[4] Canon 24 of the *Canons of Hippolytus*, which date to some time in the fourth century, instructs the deacon to let the bishop know if anyone is sick and to accompany him on his visits. The text concludes:

> It is important for the head of the presbyters to visit the sick; they are lifted out of their sickness when the bishop comes to them, and especially if he prays over them.[5]

The *Testament of Our Lord*, a fifth-century Syrian text also dependent on Hippolytus, is more expansive:

> If a priest is to consecrate oil for healing those who suffer, let him set the vessel of oil before the altar and say in a low voice: "Lord God, you have given to us the Spirit, the Paraclete, the Lord, the saving Name that is unconquerable and hidden from the foolish but revealed to the wise. Christ, you are our sanc-

[3] *Apostolic Tradition* 5.
[4] *Apostolic Constitutions* VIII, 29.
[5] D.B. de Haneberg, ed., *Canones S. Hippolyti e codicibus Romanis* (Münster, 1870).

33

tifier and you heal all sickness and suffering. Grant the gift of healing to those whom you have rendered worthy of this favor. Send upon this oil, which is an image of your abundance, the help of your merciful kindness, in order that it may set free those who suffer, heal those who are sick, and sanctify those who return, having drawn near to you in faith. For you are mighty and worthy of glory through all the ages, Amen."[6]

But the best example of a prayer over the oil comes from a fourth-century collection of prayers known as the *Prayer Book of Serapion*, whose author was an Egyptian bishop and friend of Athanasius. The collection contains three blessings of oil, one for oil and water offered by the faithful at the eucharist, a second for baptismal chrism, and a third for the oil of healing. The prayer at the eucharist seems to be intended for blessing oil to be used at home by the faithful:

We invoke you, who have all power and might, Savior of all, Father of our Lord and Savior Jesus Christ, and we pray you to send down from the heavens of your Only-begotten a curative power upon this oil, in order that to those who are anointed with these creatures or who receive them, it may become a means of removing every disease and every sickness, a warding off of every demon, of putting to flight every unclean spirit, of keeping at a distance every evil spirit, of banishing all fever, all chill, and all weariness; a means of grace and goodness and the remission of sins; a medicament of life and salvation, unto health and soundness of soul and body and spirit, unto perfect well-being.[7]

[6]*Testament of Our Lord* 1, 25.
[7]Serapion, Bishop of Thmuis in Lower Egypt, *Prayer Book of Serapion* Prayer 29.

The third prayer, however, is not only more expansive, but seems clearly to be intended for a rite of healing:

Prayer over the oil of the sick or over the bread or over the water

We call upon you who have all authority and power, O Savior of all human beings, Father of our Lord and Savior Jesus Christ, and we ask you to send healing power from the heights of heaven, from the only Son, upon this oil in order that it may remove all sickness and infirmity far from those who are anointed with it or who share in your creatures [the elements named in the title of the prayer]; that it may serve them as an antidote against every demon; that it may expel every unclean spirit from them, banish every evil spirit, dispel every fever and chill and sickness; that it may grant them good grace and forgiveness of sins; that it may be for them a remedy for life and salvation and bring them health and integrity of soul, body, and spirit, a perfect constitution. Lord, let every satanic power, every demon, every plot of the adversary, every blow, torment, or pain, every suffering or shock or disturbance or evil shadow fear your holy name which we invoke now, and the name of the only Son, so that glory may be given to the name of him who was crucified for us and was raised and took our sicknesses and infirmities upon himself: Jesus Christ who will come to judge the living and the dead. For through him may glory and power be yours in the Holy Spirit, now and through all the ages. Amen.[8]

Beyond these sources, and a few others like them, we have little information about how the rite was actually performed. Did

[8]Ibid., Prayer 33.

the faithful perform the anointing themselves? Or was it done by presbyters? Was the oil always blessed, and by whom? There clearly seems to be a number of different patterns, and this is entirely in keeping with what we now know about the tremendous variety in early Christian practice. When we look at the evidence, diverse and sparse as it is, several tendencies become evident.

First, as in both pagan and Jewish practice, the anointing of the sick seems to have originated as a domestic rite. This, of course, would certainly not preclude having presbyters assemble at the home of the sick person, as we see described in the Epistle of James. But there is no evidence of a formal liturgy of anointing the sick, while there is ample evidence in the pre-Nicene Church of the development of clear structures for baptism and eucharist. What we do see appearing here and there are prayers for blessing oil intended for anointing the sick; this is what we find in sources such as Hippolytus of Rome or Serapion of Thmuis. Most likely, the blessed oil would then be taken home, kept in the "medicine cabinet," and used as needed. The blessed oil could either be consumed or used for anointing, just as any ordinary oil would be used. The connection with the Church was the prayer of blessing pronounced over the oil by the bishop or presbyter. This domestic practice was maintained even in later centuries, when a distinct, formal rite of anointing developed. To this day, the faithful in traditionally Orthodox countries keep holy oil they obtain from lamps burning before the tombs of saints, or issuing from myrrh-gushing icons, and use it as a remedy to treat physical and spiritual ills.

At the same time, beginning in the fourth century, we also find an increasing emphasis on the role of the clergy, bishops and presbyters. Athanasius, for example, complains that, because of the

Arian persecution, the faithful remain unbaptized, and the sick are not visited.

> Moreover, there are many who while sick are visited by no one, a misfortune which they suffer not without tears, and a calamity which they regard as more bitter than sickness itself. For while the ministers of the church endure persecution, the people, who loathe the impiety of the heretical Arians, prefer to remain sick and to be in danger rather than have Arian hands laid on their head.[9]

Writing around 361, John Chrysostom, in his treatise *On the Priesthood*, stresses this in connection with the anointing of the sick:

> Not only in punishing but in doing good God has given greater power to priests than to natural parents. And the difference between them is as great as the difference between the present and the future life. For parents beget for the present life, priests for the future life; and parents cannot ward off even physical death from their children, much less guard them against virulent disease. But priests have often saved a soul that was sick and on the verge of destruction, by administering to some a milder punishment, and by preventing others from succumbing at all; and this not only by teaching and exhorting, but also by helping them with prayer. For it is not only when they regenerate [baptize] us, but even afterwards they have the power to forgive sins. "For is any among you sick?" he says. "Call in the presbyters of the church, and let them pray over him, anointing him with oil in the name of the Lord; and the prayer of faith will cure the sick man, and the

[9]Athanasius, *Encyclical Letter to the Bishops* 5 (PG 25:234).

Lord will raise him up, and if he has committed sins, it will be forgiven him."[10]

Early in the fifth century, Cyril of Alexandria witnesses to the twofold domestic and ecclesial aspects of care for the sick:

> Now if you are sick in some part of the body, and really believe that the Lord of the Sabbath and such other invocations, which Sacred Scripture attributes to God according to his nature, will be a remedy for your malady, even when you pronounce these sayings over yourself, you will do better than the pagans, since you give glory to God, and not to these impure spirits. I will also recall the divinely inspired writing which says: "Is anyone among you sick? Let him call for the presbyters of the church . . ."[11]

In the fifth century, in both East and West, there is a clear tendency to make the rite the exclusive preserve of the clergy, as the following examples show. Thus Isaac, Bishop of Antioch in the mid-fifth century, writes:

> Woman, bestow your alms on the recluse, but receive anointing from your priest; feed the monk, but let the oil you use be that of the apostles . . . and receive anointing from your priest. The servants of Christ who are orthodox make it their practice to bring their sick and infirm to the holy altar, but they do not dare administer the oil lest they seem to show contempt for the house of expiation; wherever there is a priest in charge of leading the people, the faithful observe the legitimate rules.[12]

[10]John Chrysostom, *On the Priesthood* 3, 6 (PG 48:643f).
[11]Cyril of Alexandria, *On Adoration in Spirit and in Truth* 6 (PG 68:472).
[12]G. Bickell, *Conspectus rei Syrorum litterarius* (Munich, 1871), 77–8.

In the Western Church, this increased focus on the role of the clergy leads to the requirement that only the bishop is to consecrate the oil, even though for many subsequent centuries the anointing may be performed by the faithful upon themselves.[13]

Finally, several texts point to the close connection between penance and anointing of the sick. Already in the third century, Origen quotes the passage from James 5 in a passage in which he lists the ways in which the sinner may be forgiven:

> And there is yet a seventh [way], although hard and laborious, the remission of sins through penance, when the sinner bathes his couch in tears, and his tears become his bread by day and night, and when he is not ashamed to show his sins to the priest of the Lord, and to seek the remedy. . . . In this there is fulfilled as well the saying of the Apostle James: "But if there is anyone sick, let him call for the presbyters of the church, and let them impose hands on him, anointing him with oil in the name of the Lord; and the prayer of faith will save the sick man, and if he has committed sins, they shall be forgiven him."[14]

Significant also is a text from the *Demonstration* of Aphraates, a fourth-century Syrian saint, in which he names the various uses of consecrated oil as a ("life-giving sacrament that bestows perfection on Christians, priests, kings, and prophets, brings light into darkness, anoints the sick, and brings penitents back."[15] Here, as in the text from James, healing and forgiveness

---

[13]See for example Pope Innocent's letter to Decentius, written in 416, *Epistle* 25, 8 (PL 20:559f). In Roman practice, the oil continued to be blessed at the conclusion of the eucharistic prayer, as in Hippolytus.

[14]Origen, *On Leviticus*, Homily 2.

[15]Aphraates, *Demonstatio* 23, 3.

are closely linked. Such an approach is also evident in the passages from Serapion's Prayer 33 and from John Chrysostom's *On the Priesthood* cited above. This is to become a hallmark of the eastern approach to penance and confession, in which primarily medicinal terminology is applied to the penitential process. The task of the confessor is to apply the proper medication to heal the penitent from his or her sin. Thus it is the ministry of healing which serves as the paradigm for the development of the Church's penitential discipline. We shall examine this aspect further when we examine the rites of healing more closely.

Finally, in at least some texts we see a link between anointing of the sick and the eucharist. In a number of the prayers cited above, the oil of healing is blessed at the conclusion of the anaphora. Does this also mean that the anointing of the sick was performed within the context of the eucharist? We cannot say, but Caesarius of Arles, writing in the sixth century, does seem to imply this:

> Each time a person falls sick, let him receive the body and blood of Christ and then let him anoint his body so that what is written may be proved true in him . . . [the text of James 5 follows]. Consider, my friends, that he who when sick has recourse to the Church will deserve to receive bodily health and the forgiveness of his sins. Since these two blessings can be found in the Church, why go to the enchanters?[16]

And in earliest Byzantine texts, the rite of anointing was indeed carried out within the context of the eucharistic liturgy, with the anointing following communion. The earliest western text of the full rite, dating to the ninth century, similarly has the sick person receiving communion as well as anointing.[17]

[16]Caesarius of Arles, *Sermo* 13, 3.
[17]PL 78:231–235.

* * *

Thus, while we have little evidence for how this ministry was actually carried out in the early Church, there is sufficient material to indicate that anointing and healing were indeed part of its ministry. The custom of anointing with oil, common among both pagans and Jews, was taken over, and prayers were added to make the practice expressly Christian. Further, in continuity with the descriptions in the Gospel and the Epistle of James, healing, both physical and spiritual, was closely linked with forgiveness.

The Byzantine Tradition

The earliest Byzantine liturgical manuscript containing prayers for the anointing of the sick is *Codex Barberini 336*, now located in the Vatican Library. This manuscript is the oldest extant euchologion, or priest's service book, dating to the late eighth century and containing the texts of litanies and liturgical prayers pronounced by the clergy.[18] The manuscript contains only five prayers for the rite and provides no rubrics. The first three are prayers for the sick; the last two are blessings over the oil. The first prayer, a variant of which is used today during the anointing itself, reads:

> O holy Father, physician of our souls and bodies, who sent your only-begotten Son, our Lord Jesus Christ, who heals

[18]This euchologion, with an Italian translation, has been published by S. Parenti and Elena Velkovska, eds., *L'Eucologio Barberini gr. 336* (2d ed.; Rome: Edizioni Liturgiche, 2000). This manuscript is a key witness to the practices of Hagia Sophia, the cathedral church of Constantinople. The anointing prayers are found on 195–198; 192–94 in the published text (Greek) and 350–52 (Italian translation).

every infirmity and delivers from death, through the grace of
your Christ heal also your servant (name) from the infirmities of the body which afflict him(her) and enliven him(her)
with your good will so that he(she) may thank you by fulfilling good deeds, for yours is the power, and yours is the
kingdom . . .

Interestingly, the prayer makes no mention of anointing, and in
the manuscript it appears before the prayers of consecration.
Later variants rework the text somewhat and add petitions to the
Theotokos and the saints.

The fourth prayer, little changed, is used today for consecrat-
ing the oil:

O Lord, in your mercy (*eleei*) and compassion you heal the
afflictions of our souls and bodies: sanctify now this oil
(*elaion*), O Master, that it may bring healing to those who are
anointed with it, relief from every passion, from every sickness of flesh and spirit, and from all evil, so that your holy
name may be glorified. For you are our mercy (*eleein*) and salvation, O our God, and to you belong glory . . . *to the Father*
+ to the Son, + to the Holy Spirit...

Lost in translation is the Greek play on words between oil (*elaion*)
and mercy (*eleos*). The other three prayers found in *Barberini 336*
are not used in the contemporary rite.

From the same period, we also have a brief description of the
anointing by Theodulf, Archbishop of Orléans from 798–818:

The Greeks trace the sign of the Cross with oil on the sick person three times, pouring it cross-wise from a glass vessel on
the head, the clothing, and the entire body of the sick person,
beginning the cross from the head and going down to the feet,
then from the right hand to the shoulder and across the chest

to the left hand, at each sign of the cross pronouncing: "I anoint you in the name of the Father, the Son, and the Holy Spirit, and that the Lord might raise you, and if you have sinned, your sins might be forgiven you."[19]

While the author specifies that three priests perform the anointing, he gives no other indications as to how the liturgical rite unfolded.

We thus have to wait until the eleventh century to get a fuller description. This we find in a manuscript now in the Bibliothèque Nationale in Paris, *Coislin 213*. This is a patriarchal euchology prepared in 1027 for the personal use of a presbyter assigned to Hagia Sophia, the cathedral church of Constantinople.[20] Rubrics indicate that the rite is to be performed in a domestic church[21] by seven presbyters on seven consecutive days. The following is an outline of the service:

1. The proskomide,[22] using seven prosphora.[23]

2. The blessing of oil, done by each presbyter in turn:

[19]Theodulf, Archbishop of Orléans, *Capitulare* (PL 105:221).

[20]Portions of the manuscript are reproduced in A. Dmitrievskii, *Euchologia* (vol. 2 of *Opisanie liturgicheskikh rukopisei, khraniashchikhsia v bibliotekakh pravoslavnogo vostoka*; Kiev: 1901), 993f. The rite of anointing appears on 1017–19.

[21]In medieval times, both in East and West, domestic chapels were very common. Even in Constantinople, with its many large and impressive churches, the majority of churches were in fact domestic.

[22]This is the preparatory rite of the Byzantine eucharistic liturgy, at which the bread and wine are prepared for the liturgy. On the history of this rite, see M. Mandalà, *La protesi della liturgia nel rito bizantini-greco* (Grottaferrata, 1935).

[23]The loaves of bread specially prepared for the eucharistic celebration. See G. Galavaris, *Bread and the Liturgy* (Madison: University of Wisconsin Press, 1970).

Psalm 50;

A lamp is filled with oil;

The prayer of blessing: "O Lord, in your mercy and compassion . . .";

The lamp with the blessed oil is lit.

3. The eucharistic liturgy, with a special prokeimenon, epistle, gospel,[24] koinonikon (communion verse).

4. The anointing, after the prayer before the ambo (at the conclusion of the liturgy):

Each presbyter takes some of the oil;

A troparion to the unmercenary saints is sung;[25]

Each presbyter recites the prayer of anointing, "O holy Father, physician of our souls and bodies . . . ";

Each presbyter anoints everyone in the household on the forehead, ears, chest, and hands;

As the troparion to the unmercenary saints is sung, the presbyters go through the entire house, anointing the doors, windows, and walls.

5. Conclusion of the office (in the main room of the house):

Additional troparia;

Incensation;

Gospel of the Good Samaritan (Luke 10);

Ektene (="Augmented litany");

[24]The rubrics indicate that the daily gospel may be read as well as the gospel "of the seven priests."
[25]See Appendix 1, p 132.

Dismissal.

6. Conclusion of the liturgy:

Psalm 33;

Distribution of the antidoron;

Dismissal.

If the house is wealthy, the text concludes, the clergy remain to eat. This entire rite is repeated for seven consecutive days, with a different presbyter presiding each day. During Great Lent, the Liturgy of the Presanctified Gifts replaces the regular eucharistic liturgy.

Since this text presupposes the existence of a domestic chapel, as well as the presence of seven presbyters, one wonders how commonly this rite could actually have been celebrated in this fashion. Based on other sources, however, it seems that the same rite was also celebrated in regular churches. It is also likely that, rather than using the entire rite, only individual prayers and portions of it were commonly used.[26] The practice of repeating the rite on seven consecutive days also has its counterpart in the West, specifically in a ninth-century Carolingian compilation based on Roman, Gallican, and Mozarabic sources.[27] Here, too, the communion of the sick was an integral element.

[26]This is the suggestion of M. Arranz, *Istoricheskie zametki o chino-posledovaniiakh tainstv* (Leningrad: Leningrad Theological Academy, 1979), 112.

[27]PL 78:231–6. This is similarly the oldest western full ritual. Cf. H.B. Porter, "The Origin of the Medieval Rite for Anointing the Sick or Dying," *Journal of Theological Studies* 7 (1956): 211–225. The classic work on anointing of the sick in the Latin tradition is by A. Chavasse, *Étude sur l'onction des infirmes dans l'église latine du IIe au XVe siècle* (vol. 1 of *Du IIIe siècle à la réforme carolingienne*; Lyons: 1942).

A rite similar to that in *Coislin 213*, but even more complex, appears in a twelfth-century manuscript, *Sinai gr. 973*.[28] Here again, the rite unfolds over seven consecutive days and calls for the participation of seven presbyters, though it may be done with three, or even two, if necessary. The following is an outline:

1. All seven presbyters together celebrate:

    Vespers;

    Pannychis,[29] with a special canon;

    Matins, with a special canon.

2. The eucharistic liturgy each day, celebrated by each presbyter in a different church.

3. Blessing of the oil of the sick:

    After the daily liturgy, all gather together in one church;

    The oil is prepared according to a complex rite; oil, wine, and holy water (previously blessed on Epiphany) are mixed together;

    Great Synapte (=Great Litany);

    Prayer, "For you are a great and wonderful God . . .";[30]

---

[28]Dmitrievskii, *Euchologia*, 101–9.

[29]The *pannychis* was a short cathedral vigil, usually celebrated after vespers on the eve of feasts in the practice of the Great Church of Constantinople. See M. Arranz, "Les prières presbytérales de la 'Pannychis' de l'ancien Euchologe byzantin des défunts," in *Conférences Saint-Serge: XXIIe Semaines d'Études Liturgiques 1974* (=*Ephemerides Liturgicae, Subsida 1*) (Rome: Edizione liturgiche, 1975), 31–82.

[30]J. Goar, *Euchologion* (2d ed.; Venice, 1730; repr.: Graz, 1960), 337–8. See Appendix 1, p. 137.

Ektene (=Augmented Litany);

Prayer, "O great and most-high God . . ."[31]

Each priest in turn presides over the blessing of the oil:

[Presbyter 1]

Trisagion prayers, Psalm 50, antiphon 1, penitential troparia;

Great Synapte (=Great Litany);

Prayer 1, "O Lord our God, who sit upon the cherubim . . .";[32]

The presbyter lights the lamp containing the oil.

[Presbyter 2]

Trisagion prayers, Psalm 50, antiphon 2, penitential troparia;

Prayer 2, "O Lord, our God, who in your mercies . . .";[33]

He lights the second lamp.

[Presbyter 3]

Trisagion prayers, Psalm 50, antiphon 3, penitential troparia;

Prayer 3, "Send down, O Lord, the richness of your mercy . . .";[34]

He lights the third lamp.

---

[31]Ibid., 339. See Appendix 1, p 142.

[32]Dmitrievskii, *Euchologia*, 103. This prayer is not extant in the contemporary rite.

[33]Goar, *Euchologion*, 335. See Appendix 1, p 130, the Prayer of the Oil.

[34]Dmitrievskii, *Euchologia*, 104. This prayer is no longer extant.

[Presbyter 4]

Trisagion prayers, Psalm 50, antiphon 4, penitential troparia;

Prayer 4, "We ask you, O Lord, to grant your mercy . . .",[35]

He lights the fourth lamp.

[Presbyter 5]

Trisagion prayers, Psalm 50, antiphon 5, penitential troparia;

Prayer 5, "O God of great mercy and abundant in goodness . . .",[36]

He lights the fifth lamp.

[Presbyter 6]

Trisagion prayers, Psalm 50, antiphon 6, penitential troparia;

Prayer 6, "O Lord our God, who in your mercies . . .",[37]

He lights the sixth lamp.

[Presbyter 7]

Trisagion prayers, Psalm 50, antiphon 7, penitential troparia;

Prayer 7, "O Christ our God, who are good and of great mercy . . .",[38]

He lights the seventh lamp.

[35]Ibid., 104; similar to Prayer 2 in Goar, *Euchologion*, 347.

[36]Goar, *Euchologion*, 679. This prayer is no longer used in the contemporary rite.

[37]Ibid., 335. See Appendix 1, p 130, the Prayer of the Oil.

[38]Dmitrievskii, *Euchologia*, 105. This prayer is no longer extant.

4. The eucharistic liturgy is celebrated:

   Typika antiphons (Psalms 102, 145, the Beatitudes);

   Special troparia and readings;

   Special petitions at *Ektene*;

   During the Great Entrance, the sick lie in the center of the nave.

5. Anointing follows the prayer before the ambo:

   [Presbyter 1]

   Psalm 50, prayer 1 ("O Lord our God, who in your mercies . . ."[39]), and he extinguishes his lamp.

   [Presbyter 2]

   Psalm 50, prayer 2 ("O holy Father, physician of our souls and bodies . . ."[40]), and he extinguishes his lamp.

   [Presbyter 3]

   Psalm 50, prayer 3 ("O Master almighty, holy King . . ."[41]), and he extinguishes his lamp.

   [Presbyter 4]

   Psalm 50, prayer 4 ("O Lord God, Master of all . . ."[42]), and he extinguishes his lamp.

   [Presbyter 5]

   Psalm 50, prayer 5 ("O physician of our souls and bodies . . ."[43]), and he extinguishes his lamp.

---

[39]Goar, *Euchologion*, 335. See Appendix 1, p 130, the Prayer of the Oil.
[40]Ibid., 338. See Appendix 1, p 138.
[41]Ibid., 340. See Appendix 1, p 147.
[42]Dmitrievskii, *Euchologia*, 107. No longer extant.

[Presbyter 6]

Psalm 50, prayer 6 ("O our God, the God, the God of salvation . . ."[44]), and he extinguishes his lamp.

[Presbyter 7]

Psalm 50, prayer 7 ("O holy Father, physician of our souls and bodies . . ."[45]), and he extinguishes his lamp.

Prayer of St John the Theologian ("O King, invisible, incomprehensible . . ."[46]);

Troparia to Archangel Michael and to the unmercenary saints;

Then each presbyter in turn holds the head of the sick person, recites the prayer, "O holy Father, physician of our souls and bodies,"[47] and anoints the sick person on the forehead, nostrils, chin, neck, ears, and hands;

During the anointing, the troparion to the unmercenary saints is sung;

All those present are then anointed.

6. Dismissal.

7. The sick are then escorted home, as Psalm 50 with troparia is sung antiphonally:

At each home, the sickbed, the walls, and the doors are anointed;

---

[43]Ibid., 107–8. No longer extant.
[44]Ibid., 108. No longer extant.
[45]Goar, *Euchologion*, 338. See Appendix 1, p 138.
[46]Dmitrievskii, *Euchologia*, 108–9. No longer extant.
[47]Goar, *Euchologion*, 338. See Appendix 1, p 138.

The gospel account of Zacchaeus (Luke 19.1–10) is read.

The euchology concludes the description of the rite with instructions that the sick must prepare themselves for the sacrament by confessing their sins and by washing themselves. Afterwards, they are not to wash for seven days, just like newly-baptized neophytes.

Sinai 973 marks the climax of the development of the rite. Later manuscripts show a gradual abbreviation and simplification. In the thirteenth century, anointing ceases to be celebrated in a eucharistic context, and the entire rite comes to be performed in one day. Gradually, elements from both the eucharistic liturgy and the daily office drop out, and by the fourteenth century the anointing service reaches its present form. The only reminder of its once extensive nature is the presence in the modern rite of seven scriptural units (prokeimenon, epistle, alleluia, gospel), which once belonged to the seven daily eucharistic liturgies.

The early manuscripts reveal a tremendous variety in the celebration of this sacrament, and the only constant elements are the two central prayers: the prayer of blessing over the oil ("O Lord, in your mercy and compassion . . .") and the prayer of anointing ("O holy Father, physician of souls and bodies . . ."). And even these prayers, which appear already in the earliest extant Byzantine euchology, the eighth-century *Barberini 336*, appear in several recensions.[48]

---

[48]M. Arranz, *Istoricheskie zametki*, 106–110. For more detailed studies on the development of the rite, see ibid., 103–124; M. Arkhangel'skii, *O taine sv. eleia* (St Petersburg, 1895); A Golubtsov, "Ob obriadovoi storone tainstva eleosviashcheniia," *Pribavlenie k izdaniiu tvorenii sviatykh ottsev* 42 (1888): 113–130; A. Petrovskii, "K istorii posledovaniia tainstva eleosviashcheniia," *Khristianskoe chtenie* 83 (July 1903): 44–59; "Eleosviashchenie," *Russkaia bogoslovskaia entsiklopedia* 5, cols. 397–415; Hieromonk

The Contemporary Rite

Today's service is much simpler and briefer than the elaborate rites described above. And in practice, it is typically performed with far fewer than seven presbyters and is often abbreviated. The following is an outline of the rite, whose full text appears in Appendix 1:

I. Remnants of Pannychis and Matins

- Monastic opening

- Psalm 143(142)

- Alleluia, with penitential troparia

- Psalm 50(51)

- Canon

- Exaposteilarion

- Lauds (Psalms 148–150), with stichera

- Trisagion prayers

- Concluding troparion

Benedict (Alentov), *K istorii pravoslavnago bogosluzheniia: Istoriko-liturgicheskoe i arkheologicheskoe izsledovanie o chine tainstva eleo-sviashcheniia* (Sergiev Posad, 1917); J. Dauvillier, "Extrême-onction dans les églises orientales," *Dictionnaire du droit canonique* 5 (Paris: Letouzey, 1953), cols. 725–789; E. Melia, "The Sacrament of the Anointing of the Sick: Its Historical Development and Current Practice," in *Temple of the Holy Spirit: Sickness and Death of the Christian in the Liturgy* (M.J. O'Connell, trans.; New York: Pueblo, 1983), 127–160; in the same volume, see also articles by C. Andronikov, A. Kniazeff, P. Kovalevsky, G. Wagner. A more complete bibliography can be found in A.M. Triacca, "Per una rassegna sul sacramento dell'Unzione degli infermi," *Ephemerides liturgicae* 89 (1975): 397–467, esp. 429–433.

II. Blessing of Oil

- Litany, with special petitions

- Oil and wine poured into containers

- Prayer of blessing ("O Lord, in your mercy and compassion . . .")

- Troparia

III. Anointing (repeated seven times as a unit)

- Prokeimenon

- Epistle

- Alleluia

- Gospel

- Ektene and collect

- Anointing and prayer ("O holy Father, physician of our souls and bodies . . .")

IV. Absolution

- Gospel book placed over head of sick person

- Prayer of absolution recited by first priest

V. Dismissal

- Concluding litany

- Apolytikia (dismissal troparia)

- Dismissal

Part I, which resembles the contemporary service of matins, in fact consists of an abbreviated pannychis[49] together with remnants of the conclusion of matins (the exaposteilarion and the

[49]See n 29 above.

stichera on the Lauds). The canon, first specifically mentioned in *Sinai 973*,[50] was clearly composed to accompany a rite of anointing and is ascribed to Arsenius, a ninth-century archbishop of Corfu and a friend of Patriarch Photius.[51]

Part II contains the blessing of oil, now removed from its original place at the beginning of the eucharistic liturgy.

Part III, the anointing, repeated sevenfold, retains the prokeimena, epistles, alleluia verses, and gospels from what had been the seven daily eucharistic liturgies, combining them with the anointings. The scriptural readings, so intimately tied to the meaning of the anointing of the sick, have been retained. But since the celebration of the eucharist no longer follows, the anointing now comes not at the conclusion of the eucharist but directly after each set of readings, accompanied by the ancient prayer of anointing ("O holy Father, physician of our souls and bodies . . .").

Part IV consists of a prayer of absolution, during which the gospel book is placed over the head of sick person. This prayer first appears in this context in the thirteenth-century manuscript, *Athos Lavra 189*. During the recitation of the prayer, the presbyters are instructed to lay their hands on the head of the sick person (as the text of the prayer still indicates). Beginning in the fourteenth century, placing the gospel book over the head replaced the actual laying on of hands.[52] The prayer is a reworking of a penitential prayer that already appears among the prayers for the rite of penance in the eighth-century euchologion, *Barberini 336*.[53]

---

[50]Though it is likely that the same canon was used in the 11th-century *Coislin 213* as well.

[51]Hieromonk Benedict (Alentov), *K istorii*, 119.

[52]In the Athonite euchologion, *Koutloumousiou 491* (Dmitrievskii, *Euchologia*, 353). Interestingly, the prayer still refers to a laying on of hands.

[53]Parenti and Velkovska, *L'Eucologio Barberini gr. 336*, f. 228, 221–2.

Part V, the dismissal, is a typical monastic conclusion to an office.

Thus a service that was once spread over seven consecutive days, that incorporated both a full daily cycle of prayer and the eucharistic liturgy, has been abbreviated to the present rite, albeit one that still takes several hours if done in its entirety.

The Celebration of the Rite

Studying the development of the structures and texts certainly gives some idea of how the rite was celebrated over the centuries, but it does not provide a full picture. We can learn only so much from manuscripts. Most contain few rubrics. They do not indicate whether the texts were used as written, or abbreviated. Nor, in most cases, do we learn when the rite was performed, or how often. And whereas rites such as baptism and the eucharist, at least in their basic shape, were fixed early in the Church's history, the rite of anointing continued to develop for a much longer time. In addition, it never became a part of a regular cycle of services, but was used when needed, at different times and places, to meet particular needs.

One needs only to examine contemporary practice to see the variety that exists. We find two basic patterns, Greek and Slavic. Greek practice is followed by all the Greek-speaking churches, as well as the Patriarchate of Antioch and those churches which are influenced by modern Greek practice, such as the Orthodox Church of Albania. Slavic practice is generally followed by the Orthodox Churches of Slavic origin, including Russian, Ukrainian, Serbian, Bulgarian, and others. A few churches, such as the Romanian, are influenced by both traditions and thus reflect a variety of practices. This is particularly the case in America, where both traditions exist side by side, and where practices vary from parish to parish, even within the same jurisdiction.

Greek Practice

The most common celebration of the sacrament of anointing in Greek practice is during Holy Week, typically on Holy Wednesday afternoon or evening. This is one of the most popular services of the entire year, and churches are filled to the brim. In the United States and Canada, the service typically replaces the matins of Holy Thursday.[54] In Greece, the rite is often celebrated during the other fasting periods as well, particularly before Christmas. All the faithful are anointed once at the conclusion of the long service. The primary purpose of the rite here is to prepare for paschal communion, though the popular literature justifies the practice by affirming that everyone is in need of both physical and spiritual healing. Often, the sacrament is understood simply as a "general service of blessing,"[55] or as a replacement for confession—this is particularly the case in North America, where private confession is all but unknown in the vast majority of Greek parishes.[56]

---

[54]The matins of Holy Thursday is normally celebrated on Wednesday evening, in anticipation, as are all the services of Holy Week.

[55]Cf. Stanley Harakas, *Health and Medicine in the Eastern Orthodox Tradition* (New York: Crossroad, 1990), 106.

[56]The reasons for this are complex, but they are largely due to the fact that Greek faithful in Greece typically confess to a monastic elder, and not to their parish priest. Unlike Greece, America has few monasteries, and this has led to the virtual disappearance of confession among Greek Orthodox communities.

This practice of general anointing appears quite early. Already in the eleventh century, *Coislin 213*, which contains the first full description of the rite, indicates that all the faithful were anointed on the day commemorating St Theodore of Tyre (the first Saturday of Great Lent) and on Lazarus Saturday (the day before Palm Sunday).[57] A twelfth-century *Typikon* given by the Empress Irene at the founding of a convent in 1118 similarly indicates that all the nuns should be anointed on Lazarus Saturday.[58] In the thirteenth century, Pope Innocent IV forbids this practice among Greeks in Cyprus who had just concluded a union with Rome.[59] By the seventeenth century, the general anointing was usually performed on Holy Thursday or Holy Saturday. There is also evidence at this time for the same practice in Russia.[60] The service was conducted with particular solemnity at the Cathedral of the Dormition in Moscow and at the Trinity-St Sergius Monastery, the two major centers of Russian liturgical life, into the twentieth century, though the practice died out elsewhere. Interestingly, the modern liturgical books, the *Typikon*,[61] the *Triodion*,[62] whether Greek or Russian, show no trace of this practice. The sacrament of anointing has remained outside the regular cycles of worship,

[57]Dmitrievskii, *Euchologia*, 1018.

[58]F. Miklosich and I. Müller, *Acta et diplomata monasterium et Ecclesiarum Orientis* (Vienna, 1888), V (II): 379.

[59]Pope Innocent IV, *Epist. 6, Ad Ottonem cardinalem Tusculanum*, March 6, 1254 (Mansi XXIII, 580).

[60]Cf. N. Krasnoseltsev, "Obshchee maslosviashchenie v velikii chetvertok ili v velikiu subbotu," *Pravoslavnyi Sobesednik* (1887): 89ff. See also B. Alentov, *K istorii*, 39.

[61]The *Typikon* regulates the use of all the Orthodox liturgical books, containing more or less precise rubrics for every day of the year.

[62]The *Triodion* contains the variable portions of services during Great Lent through Holy Week.

celebrated whenever needed or desired. This is the rule to this day. Among the Greek Orthodox, families will often request the service to be celebrated at their home, whether because a family member is ill, simply as a general service of blessing, or in conjunction with penance.[63]

The purpose of celebrating this general anointing a short time before Pascha seems to be connected with preparation for the reception of communion at this climactic feast of the church year. Already in the third century, Pascha became the normal time for the celebration of baptism, which concluded with the neophytes receiving communion for the first time at the paschal eucharist. Ever since the period of public penance[64] in the third and fourth centuries, Holy Thursday was often the day on which public penitents were reconciled to the Church and restored to communion. It is significant in this regard that, early on, penance was understood and even referred to as "second baptism." There are even some indications that at one time chrism, traditionally blessed by the bishop on Holy Thursday, was used not only for those undergoing baptism, but also to anoint penitents who were being reconciled. The fact that the gospel reading for Holy Thursday also mentions the anointing of Christ before the Last Supper by the

---

[63]See the study of contemporary Greek practice by B. Groen, "The Anointing of the Sick in the Greek Orthodox Church," *Concilium* 4 (1991): 50–59.

[64] Before the development of today's practice of private confession, penance was a public affair, lasting several years. After years of penance, during which persons who had committed major sins (apostasy, murder, adultery . . .) were excluded from participation in the eucharist, sinners were publicly reconciled to the Church. On the development of the practice of confession in the Orthodox Church, see J. Erickson, "Penitential Discipline in the Orthodox Canonical Tradition," in *The Challenge of Our Past* (Crestwood, NY: SVS Press, 1991), 23–38.

sinful woman may have contributed to this development. Indeed, Great Lent, though it originated with the preparation of catechumens for baptism on Pascha, subsequently changed into a period of preparation for Pascha for penitents, and eventually for all Christians.[65] This preparation included fasting, almsgiving, and, increasingly, confession of sins. All this no doubt had an impact on the practice of anointing the sick; and, since approximately the twelfth century, sick persons were expected to confess their sins prior to the service of anointing. This seems a natural development, given the close connection between sickness and sin, between the rites of anointing the sick and of penance and confession, though it raises some questions which will be discussed in chapter four.

Slavic Practice

The practice in Russia was, until the seventeenth century, essentially the same as in the Greek churches. The requirement that seven priests carry out the rite, taken literally among the liturgically conservative Slavs, meant that the full rite could be performed only in large monasteries or cathedrals, where there was a sufficient number of clergy. As a result, the rite comes to be celebrated less and less frequently. Of even more significant impact, however, was the latinizing theology of Metropolitan Peter Moghila of Kiev (+1646). Educated by the Jesuits in Poland according to the Latin, scholastic method of the day, he published a series of liturgical books which incorporated this different

---

[65]On the development of Great Lent, see particularly A. Schmemann, *Great Lent: Journey to Pascha* (Crestwood, NY: SVS Press, 1969). On baptism, see his *Of Water and the Spirit* (Crestwood, NY: SVS Press, 1974).

approach. His most significant liturgical work was the *Trebnik*[66] (Kiev, 1646), which contained not only the texts of the services, but also explanatory articles of his own composition. It is in these articles that his latinizing tendency is most clear.[67]

The Latin practice of Peter Moghila's day had reduced the anointing of the sick to "extreme unction," to be performed only upon the approach of death.[68] Though Peter did not go quite this far, he insisted that the rite should be performed only upon the sick person, and only in the case of grievous illness. He did state that the rite could be repeated, though not for the same illness. For all intents and purposes, however, the anointing of the sick soon became understood as extreme unction, administered only upon the approach of death. The anointing of all those attending, common in Slavic liturgical books through the first half of the seventeenth century, was criticized by Moghila and eventually disappeared. His approach to the sacrament was incorporated in the 1671 *Trebnik* published in Moscow and has regulated Russian practice ever since. The other Slavic churches, dependent upon the Muscovite liturgical editions, followed suit.

In late-nineteenth-century Russia, the question was again brought up in the context of the revival of patristic and liturgical study. Scholars became aware that the existing practice was a recent innovation and did not reflect the Orthodox tradition. The

[66]The *Trebnik* ("Book of Needs") is the Slavonic version of the Greek *Euchologion*, or priest's service book, containing the prayers and litanies for the daily cycle, the eucharist, all the sacraments, and assorted blessings.

[67]On Moghila's latinizing tendencies, see my article: "The Liturgical Reforms of Peter Moghila, A New Look," *St Vladimir's Theological Quarterly* 29 (1985): 101–114.

[68]This practice developed in the West during the Carolingian era (*9th* c.) and was officially formulated at the Council of Florence (1438–39) and confirmed at the Council of Trent (*16th* c.). It was reversed following Vatican II.

question of a return to earlier practice was even on the agenda of the Moscow Council of 1917, but the Bolshevik Revolution prevented this council from doing much more than restoring the patriarchate and electing Tikhon to the position.

Orthodoxy in the West

The Orthodox living in the "West," whether in the Americas or Western Europe, have brought with them whatever practices they inherited, whether Greek or Slavic. In this new context, diverse traditions exist side by side, and they have begun to influence one another. It is increasingly common for churches following the Slavic tradition, for example, to celebrate the unction service on Holy Wednesday, just as among parishes of the Greek or Antiochian archdioceses. In some cases, parishes from different jurisdictions come together several times a year, or even monthly, for joint unction services, to which the sick from all the different communities are brought together. For the most part, the understanding of the sacrament as extreme unction has been replaced with a broader understanding that it benefits all who are sick. At such common services, sometimes only the sick are anointed; at other times all in attendance are anointed as well. The explanation given for the general anointing is that all are in need of healing.

The situation in the West clearly calls for and allows for some creative solutions. Here, there is a greater openness to change, as well as the possibility for revitalizing a sacrament that is an essential aspect of the Church's mission. We shall have more to say on this in the pastoral conclusion to this book.

CHAPTER 3

Theology of the Rite of Anointing

The rite of anointing is not familiar to most Orthodox Christians, who rarely if ever experience it in its entirety. In some Orthodox traditions, the rite is celebrated only once a year, in greatly abbreviated form, on Wednesday of Holy Week. On those rare occasions when the rite is performed over a sick person, it is usually abbreviated as well, and few of the faithful are typically present. The experience of sickness has thus been almost entirely removed from its proper place in the life of the Church. Sickness and healing are seen primarily as the responsibility of the medical profession, the doctors, the hospitals, and the health care industry. Yet the anointing rite has much to tell us about the Christian understanding of illness, and it is to this that we now turn.

By its sheer length, by the interplay of so many themes and elements, and because it is so rarely celebrated, the rite of anointing may indeed at first glance seem confusing. The rite constantly refers not only to physical and spiritual illness, but also to sin. What, then, is the connection between sickness and sin? While physical healing is certainly an important element of the rite, it is certainly not its only aim. If it were, then the true test of the rite would be only whether the sick person regained physical health. Healing, however, consists of far more than the restoration of physical health. For if restoration of physical health were the sole or primary goal, then the Church would have little to add to the marvels of modern medicine. What, also, is the connection between the rite of anointing and the Church? The answers to these and other questions can be found by looking more closely at what the rite itself has to say.

Sickness and Sin

> . . . the prayer of faith will save the sick man, and the Lord will raise him up; and if he has committed sins, he will be forgiven. Therefore confess your sins to one another, and pray for one another, that you may be healed. (Jas 5.15–16)

For us today, perhaps the most striking aspect of the rite of healing is the frequent connection made between sickness and sin, between healing and forgiveness. This is evident throughout the rite, in the scriptural readings, in the hymns, as well as in the prayers. Very often, sickness and sin are mentioned in the same breath, almost as though the sickness of the individual was caused directly by the sins that he or she had committed. The answer, of course, is not quite so simple.

It is a fundamental Christian belief that suffering and sickness are the consequence of sin. The creation narrative in Genesis makes it clear that humanity was created to dwell in paradise, in the company of God, where, in the words of the funeral kontakion, there is no "sickness and sorrow." As a result of the sin committed by Adam and Eve, however, humanity was expelled from paradise, and the consequence of their actions was sickness, suffering, and death. Sickness, suffering, and death, therefore, are not normal. Humanity was created not for suffering and death, but for eternal life in communion with God. As a result of human sin, however, this communion has been broken; and the physical consequences of this break are sickness and death, because apart from God there can be no life, but only death. It is only in this world that sickness and death reign, and one has only to turn on the television or read a newspaper to see the evidence.

We live in a world that is out of joint. In biblical terms, our world is under the dominion of the prince of this world, the devil. The inescapable conclusion is that we all sin, we all suffer, and we all die. We are utterly powerless to stop this vicious cycle, and this is amply evident in human history, whether ancient or modern. Indeed, the twentieth century was by far the bloodiest in history, and there seems little improvement in the early years of the twenty-first. Epidemics, disease, strife, suffering—all remain despite the remarkable progress in technology, science, and medicine. Despite all of society's efforts to conceal this harsh reality from us, it is always ultimately revealed, whether in very visible tragedies such as the massacres in Rwanda, the destruction of the World Trade Center in New York,[1] massive earthquakes, floods, and tsunamis in many parts of the world, or in the sickness, suffering, and death that each of us inevitably faces, often alone. We are in the midst of a great cosmic battle between good and evil. This battle is fought on many fronts, whether in the power struggles between nations, in our social and family lives, or in the depths of our own hearts.

"Thy kingdom come." One day, as we constantly beseech in the Lord's Prayer, Christ will return, the kingdom will come, and

[1]September 11, 2001.

all things will be restored to their proper order. Sin, death, and suffering will be swept away and peace will reign. In the words of Isaiah, "The wolf shall dwell with the lamb, and the leopard shall lie down with the kid."[2] This is the work inaugurated by Christ, but it will be completed only when he returns again, this time in power and glory, to judge the world and to reveal the kingdom in all its fullness. The ultimate victory of Christ is assured, but as long as we remain in this fallen world, sin, suffering, sickness, and death will continue.

Yet in the Church, particularly in the liturgy, we get a foretaste of the life of the kingdom. We are made members of the Church through baptism, by which we are cleansed of our sins and become, by adoption, sons of God and heirs of the kingdom. Every Sunday, we gather together in the eucharistic liturgy, sharing in Christ's body and blood and thus realizing our membership in Christ's body, the Church. It is here, in baptism and in the Eucharist, that we become the community of saints, "a chosen race, a royal priesthood, a holy nation, God's own people."[3] Our citizenship is now in heaven. But while our true home is the kingdom, we remain for a while in this world, where darkness, sin, and sickness still rule.

In the rite of anointing, this situation is taken for granted, and in nearly every case, sin and sickness are mentioned together, as the following examples clearly indicate:

O Physician and Helper of the suffering, O Redeemer and Savior of the sick, O Master and Lord of all, grant healing to your ailing servant. Show compassion, have mercy on him(her) who has grievously sinned, and deliver him(her)

[2]Isa 11.6.
[3]1 Pet 2.9.

from his(her) sins, that he(she) may glorify your divine power.[4]

Come and abide in your servant (name), who acknowledges his(her) sins, and who in faith draws near to you. Accept him(her) in your love for humanity, forgive him(her) if he(she) has sinned in word, deed, or thought, cleanse him(her), purify him(her) from every sin. Ever abide with him(her), protect him(her) all the remaining years of his(her) life, so that, ever walking in your commandments, he(she) may not again become an object of scorn for the devil, and so that your most-holy Name may be glorified in him(her).[5]

On this holy day and at this hour, and at every time and place, O exceedingly good King, incline your ear to my prayer and receive the voice of my supplication: grant healing to your servant (name), who lies in sickness of both soul and body, grant him(her) forgiveness of his(her) sins and pardon of his(her) transgressions, both voluntary and involuntary. Heal his(her) incurable wounds, and every disease, and all infirmity. Grant healing to his(her) soul, as you touched Peter's mother-in-law, and the fever left her, and she arose and served you. Grant also healing to your servant (name), and release from all deadly suffering, O Master, remembering your abundant compassion and mercy. Remember that the human mind always inclines toward evil, even from youth, and that no one sinless is to be found upon the earth; for you alone are sinless, who came down and saved the human race and freed us from bondage to the enemy. For if you enter into judgment with your servant, no one shall be found without stain, but every

[4]Second Kathisma hymn, tone 4.
[5]Prayer of the second priest.

mouth shall be sealed, unable to offer excuse; for before you our righteousness is like a cast-off rag. Therefore do not remember the offenses of our youth, O Lord, for you are the hope of the hopeless, the repose of those who labor and are weighed down with sin; and to you we give glory, together with your Father, who is without beginning, and your all-holy, good, and life-giving Spirit: now and ever, and unto ages of ages.[6]

Indeed, the seven long prayers read by the priests before they each anoint the sick person focus more on sin than they do on physical illness. The link between sin and sickness sometimes seems so strong that there seems to be an almost causal relationship between the two. Thus a sick person might think that it is his or her own sin that caused the sickness. But, again, the reality is not so simple.

In some cases, it is easy to see a direct connection between the two. There are certainly times when we cause our sickness by the choices we make. A person who smokes several packs of cigarettes a day will likely develop either emphysema or lung cancer. One who engages in promiscuous or homosexual sex may very well contract AIDS or other sexually transmitted diseases. Those of us who eat or drink too much contribute to the liver or heart ailments we develop.

At other times, however, the connection is not so clear or direct. A newborn with cancer has certainly done nothing sinful to contribute to its illness. Nor has a child with hemophilia who gets AIDS through a blood transfusion. In no way can it be said that they are guilty of any sins, nor that the disease comes as a punishment for such sins. In this regard, the Orthodox position is

[6]Prayer of the fifth priest.

strikingly different from the classical western view that sees original sin as inherited guilt and sickness and death as divine punishment. In this western approach, based on the theology of Augustine, each of us is guilty of Adam's sin, and thus each of us deserves punishment. Sickness and death, therefore, are understood to be the punishment we all deserve. For the Orthodox, on the other hand, sickness and suffering are the inevitable consequence of the sinful state of the whole world, which followed upon the sin committed by Adam and Eve. Sickness, suffering, and death are the inevitable result of the separation between God and humanity that took place when humanity disobeyed God's command, when it chose to please itself rather than God. Sickness, suffering, and death are the lot of all humanity in this fallen world—we all share the same fate, saint and sinner, young and old. Even Jesus Christ, who was totally without sin, shared our fate when he condescended to suffer and die—this is the very essence of the mystery of the incarnation.

The Orthodox see the fall as a kind of infection that has, through the original sin, spread to all humanity, and, through humanity, to the whole world.[7] In each of us, the process of disease, decay, and ultimately death begins from the very moment that we are conceived. When we sin, moreover, we contribute to a process that is already underway in each of us. This is the state of the world in which we live, and this is the sad reality that the Son of God came to overcome.

---

[7]For a fuller treatment of the connection between sickness and original sin, see Jean-Claude Larchet, *The Theology of Illness* (Crestwood, NY: SVS Press, 2002), especially 26–39. A more technical discussion of the origin of the interpretation of sin as original guilt can be found in John Meyendorff, "'*Eph'ô* chez Cyrille d'Alexandrie et Theodoret," *Studia Patristica* 4 (1961): 157–161.

Ultimately, the result of Adam's fall, the result of our own fall when we choose sin, is alienation—alienation first of all from God, but also from others, from the world, and even from ourselves.[8] This is something we all experience in our own lives, sooner or later.

The Experience of Sickness

Nothing brings this reality into greater starkness than when we fall ill. In sickness, our physical and emotional integrity is disrupted. The ailing body comes to the forefront of consciousness. Rather than being subject to the self, the body is enslaved by an alien, pathological force. The ailing body becomes the controlling factor in our life. This results in the disruption of emotional harmony, in anxiety about the future, anxiety about those to and for whom we are responsible. We can no longer live life as we have up to now. This experience is presented in striking terms by the Russian writer, Leo Tolstoy, in his short novel, *The Death of Ivan Ilich*.

Ivan Ilich is a moderately wealthy, influential person, a judge in a provincial Russian city. His life is entirely conventional. He is married, has children, and his whole life is his work. He sees himself as a "good person." In all these aspects, he is little different from the typical middle-class American or European of today. But then he develops a disease, a pain in his side which will not

---

[8]In the following section, I summarize the excellent article on this subject by M.J. Glen, "Sickness and Symbol: The Promise of the Future," *Worship* 54 (1980): 396–411. See also my article, "The Anointing of the Sick: Some Pastoral Considerations," *SVTQ* 35 (1991): 241–255.

go away, and which grows progressively worse. He goes from doctor to doctor, tries different cures, but nothing helps. Eventually, he comes to the realization that he may die, and at first he tries to deny this:

> And he was unable to understand, and tried to dispel this thought as being false, irregular, and morbid, and to substitute for it other, regular, healthy thoughts. But this thought,—not merely thought, but, as it were, reality,—came back and stood before him.
>
> And he invoked in the place of this thought other thoughts in rotation, in the hope of finding a support in them. He tried to return to his former trains of thought, which heretofore had veiled the thought of death from him. But, strange to say, what formerly had veiled, concealed, and destroyed the consciousness of death, now could no longer produce this effect. Of late, Ivan Ilich passed the greater part of his time in these endeavours to reestablish his former trains of feeling, which had veiled death from him.
>
> He said to himself, "I will busy myself with my service, for have I not lived by it heretofore?" and he went to court, dispelling all doubts from himself; he entered into conversation with his associates, and seated himself in his customary manner, casting a distracted, pensive glance upon the crowd, and leaning with both his emaciated hands on the rests of the oak chair, leaning over to an associate, as on former occasions, moving up the case, and whispering, and then, suddenly casting an upward glance and seating himself straight, he pronounced the customary words and began the case. But suddenly, in the middle, the pain in his side, paying no attention to the period of development of this case, began its own,

gnawing work. Ivan Ilich listened to it and dispelled the thought of it, but it continued its work and came and stationed itself right in front of him and looked at him, and he was dazed, and the fire went out in his eyes, and he began to ask himself again, "Is it possible *it* alone is true?" And his associates and his men under him saw in surprise and sorrow that he, such a brilliant and shrewd judge, was getting mixed up and making blunders. He shook himself, tried to come back to his senses, and somehow managed to bring the session to a close, and returned home with the sad consciousness that his judicial work could not, as it had done of old, conceal from him what he wished to be concealed, and that by means of his judicial work he could not be freed from *it*. And, what was worst of all, was this, that *it* drew him toward itself, not that he might be able to do something, but only that he might look at it, straight into its eyes,—that he might look at it and, without doing anything, might suffer unutterably.

And, while trying to escape this state, Ivan Ilich sought consolation and other shields, and the other shields appeared and for a short time seemed to save him, but soon they were again, not destroyed, but made transparent, as though *it* penetrated through everything, and nothing could shroud *it*.[9]

As Ivan's disease progressed, he was no longer able to pretend that it did not exist or that he could go on living as before. His physical suffering grew, but the physical suffering was less than the spiritual suffering that accompanied it:

How it all happened in the third month of Ivan Ilich's disease is hard to tell, because it all happened imperceptibly step by

[9]Leo Tolstoy, *The Death of Ivan Ilich*, 49–50.

step, but what happened was that his wife and his son, and the servants, and his acquaintances, and the doctors, and, above all else, he himself knew that the whole interest in him consisted for others in nothing but the question how soon he would vacate the place, would free the living from the embarrassment produced by his presence, and would himself be freed from his sufferings.

He slept less and less: he was given opium, and they began to inject morphine into him. But this did not make it easier for him. The dull dejection which he experienced in his half-sleeping state at first gave him relief as something new, but later it grew to be the same, and even more agonizing, than the sharp pain.[10]

Ivan keeps reviewing his past life to try to understand what is happening to him. Is he being punished for something he has done? But no—he has led a good life.

"It is impossible to resist," he said to himself. "But if I only understood what it is all for. And this is impossible. One might be able to explain it, if it could be said that I had not lived properly. But that can by no means be asserted," he said to himself, as he recalled all the lawfulness, regularity, and decency of his life. "It is impossible to admit this," he said to himself, smiling with his lips, as though someone could see this smile of his and be deceived by it. "There is no explanation! Torment, death—Why?"[11]

Two weeks later, his condition worsens further:

The doctor arrived at the usual hour. Ivan Ilich answered him,

[10]Ibid., 52.
[11]Ibid., 73.

"Yes, no," without taking his glance of fury from him, and finally said:

"You know yourself that nothing will help me, so let it go."

"We can alleviate your suffering," said the doctor.

"You cannot do that, either,—let it go."

The doctor went into the drawing-room and informed Praskovya Fedorovna [Ivan's wife] that he was in a very bad state, and that there was only one means,—opium,—in order to alleviate the sufferings, which must be terrible.

The doctor said that his physical suffering was terrible, and that was true; but more terrible than his physical suffering was his moral suffering, and in this lay his chief agony.[12]

As death approaches, Ivan will still not let go, though he does come to the realization that his whole life has been a lie, which only increases his pain. As was the case with Leo Tolstoy himself, Ivan sees little positive in Orthodox Christianity, and he suffers alone, unable and unwilling to accept the assistance and consolation the Church has to offer. Nevertheless, through the pathetic figure of Ivan, Tolstoy presents an extremely accurate picture of the human condition and the experience of sickness in all its dimensions.

As is evident from this account, illness leads to alienation from others. There is the physical segregation from human society, whether one is home in bed, or in a hospital or other institution. Even in the company of others, the sick person typically feels isolated and alone. "The sheer physical and emotional energy required for survival and adaptation may leave him with few

[12]Ibid., 74–5.

resources with which to relate to them."[13] The sick person feels that he or she has little in common with healthy people, no common sphere of existence.

Illness also brings a shift in roles: whatever their social status and function before, sick persons now become totally dependent on others. Particularly in the case of prolonged illness, the patient can regress emotionally—"by refusing to make decisions, by demanding care and seeking security in maternalistic or paternalistic attention from the deliverers of care."[14]

Sick persons are often reduced to the status of a dependent child. They begin to doubt that they can contribute to the lives of others, particularly to those to whom they were close before. This often leads to guilt, because we live in a society where productivity has become the measure of human worth. There may also be guilt because they may question the extent to which they may have caused the disease in the first place.[15]

The one who falls sick thus is depersonalized:

> He does in fact experience himself as an object on multiple levels: on the personal level, he becomes the object rather than the subject of his body; on the community level, he becomes the object of care and concern; and in the health care setting, he becomes the object of diagnosis and treatment.[16]

He is treated as a mechanism which is broken down and needs repair (or is beyond repair). In modern medicine, "quality of life" is often not an issue—machines can keep a heart beating almost indefinitely. Modern medical advances have made longevity the

---

[13]M.J. Glen, "Sickness and Symbol," 399.
[14]Ibid, 400.
[15]Ibid, 400–401.
[16]Ibid, 401.

norm in industrialized societies, but little thought has been given to the spiritual implications. Contemporary medicine treats only the body, and only in recent years have medical professionals become aware of the spiritual dimensions of both health and sickness. This is something the Church has known for a long time.[17] Indeed, the first hospitals were founded in the fourth century by Eastern Christian bishops and monks![18] The Church continued to be the chief sponsor of hospitals in subsequent centuries, in some cases down to the present.[19]

Given the present state of medical care, it is hardly surprising that sick persons experience alienation from God as well. They are often unable to come to church. They may even blame God for their illness. The very meaning of their life seems lost, and this often leads to spiritual collapse.[20] Often for the first time, they become aware of their own mortality. In short, they come face to face with the horrible reality of this fallen world, where sin, sickness, and death rule. This is the reality that Jesus came into the world to conquer, and, in Christ, our own victory is assured as well.

Our contemporary world, however, seeks at all costs to conceal this reality. Our culture idolizes beauty and youth in a vain attempt to conceal the ravages of sickness and sin. We acquire

[17]See, for example, S. Harakas, *Health and Medicine in the Eastern Orthodox Tradition.*

[18]D. Constantelos, *Byzantine Philanthropy and Social Welfare* (New Brunswick, NJ: Rutgers University Press, 1968); T. Miller, *The Birth of the Hospital in the Byzantine Empire* (Baltimore: Johns Hopkins University Press, 1985).

[19]The St Joseph Hospital in Beirut is sponsored by the Orthodox Church in Lebanon. Similarly, in the West, the Roman Catholic and other churches sponsor numerous hospitals.

[20]J.M. Glen, "Sickness and Symbol," 401–403.

wealth and power in a futile attempt to stave off the inevitable. We send our sick off to sterile, antiseptic hospitals and institutions not simply in order to heal them, but to keep them out of sight. We pack our aged off to what we euphemistically call "senior citizen homes." When our family members die, we ship them to funeral homes that embalm and prepare the bodies to make them look as though they are still alive. Or we hold funerals with closed caskets—all in order to avoid seeing death face to face. We do all these things precisely because we wish at all costs to avoid seeing the reality of this fallen, sinful world.

The reality is that all these things are closely interconnected. Physical sickness is but one external manifestation of a spiritual reality. Sickness, therefore, is never purely physical, but always has a spiritual dimension as well. Just as sin can cause sickness and death, so also sickness can lead to sin. Modern medicine thus often falls short precisely because it attempts to treat the physical disease in isolation from all its other manifestations. Modern medicine seeks to heal the body alone, seeks to keep the biological processes functioning as long as possible, all too often paying little attention to the quality and purpose of life. Ultimately, modern medicine often denies its own limitations, refusing to see that any success is only temporary—eventually, even those who are cured will get physically sick again and die.

Healing

Because sickness is such a complex reality, healing is as well. The service of anointing directly addresses this complex reality. We pray, first of all, for physical healing. But that is not the most important thing. We pray also for spiritual healing and forgiveness, without which any physical healing is meaningless. As part of the spiritual healing, we pray for the reintegration of the ailing person into the body of the Church, into fullness of life, whatever the ultimate course of the physical disease. This is because the ultimate aim of Christian healing is nothing less than the restoration of full communion with God, which is the aim of all human existence. The ultimate goal is the kingdom of God—that is the meaning of salvation.

> You commanded the sick to summon the godly ministers, to obtain salvation through their prayers and anointing with your oil: O loving God, by your mercy save your suffering servant.[21]

All these themes are woven together in this long and complex ritual.

Physical Healing

Certainly, physical healing is desirable, and it is repeatedly asked for in the rite. At the same time, the rite is not intended to replace professional medical care, and the Church is well aware that God works through the medical profession as well, that he has endowed humanity with intelligence and the ability to develop the art of healing. This comes from the knowledge that God created the world, that he gave us the breath of life, and that he is the ultimate source of all healing. Medical doctors themselves are aware that it is not they themselves who heal—their task is to aid in the healing process by all the tools at their disposal. However, they do not have ultimate control over what happens. Some peo-

---

[21]Canon, Ode 4, Troparion.

---

ple respond well to treatment, while others do not. Some experience what can only be described as miraculous recoveries, for which the medical profession has no explanation. In other words, all healing, including physical healing, is *always* a gift from God, even when it is mediated through health care providers.

Numerous texts in the rite refer to physical healing, though usually in connection to the healing of the soul and spirit as well:

O Master almighty, holy King, you chastise but do not kill; you raise the fallen and restore those who are cast down; you relieve our bodily afflictions: we beg you, O our God, to direct your mercy upon this oil, and upon all who shall be anointed with it in your Name, that it may be for the healing of their souls and bodies, for purification, and for the removal of every passion, every disease and infirmity, and every defilement of body and spirit. Yea, Lord, send down from heaven your healing power: touch the bodies; quench the fever; ease the suffering; and drive away every hidden ailment. Be the physician of your servant (name): raise him(her) up from his(her) bed of sickness, from the bed of affliction, whole and fully cured, granting him(her), through your Church, that which is well-pleasing to you and accomplishes your will.[22]

Stretch forth your hand from on high, O Loving God; and having blessed your oil, O Savior, bestow it on your servant for healing and for a release of all ills.[23]

In your mercy and compassion, O only God and Savior, you heal both the passions of the soul and the failings of the body: restore also this suffering servant and heal him(her).[24]

[22]Prayer of the third priest.
[23]Canon, ode 6, troparion.
[24]Canon, ode 7, troparion.

As can be seen from these examples, physical healing implies not just the healing of the body, but of the soul as well. This is most evident in the prayer over the oil, a central prayer in the rite recited by each of the priests performing the rite:

> O Lord, in your mercy and compassion, you heal the afflic-tions of our souls and bodies: sanctify now this oil, O Master, that it may bring healing to those who are anointed with it, relief from every passion, from every sickness of flesh and spirit, and from all evil; and so that your holy name may be glorified, of the Father, and of the Son, and of the Holy Spirit, now and ever, and unto ages of ages.

The prayers that precede each of the seven anointings simi-larly weave together the themes of physical and mental healing, as well as the forgiveness of sins. This puts physical healing in its proper perspective—not as an end in itself, but so that the body may be used for the purpose for which it was created: to glorify God, to hasten the coming of the kingdom, to witness to the truth of Christ in the Gospel.

Spiritual Healing

Within the rite, physical and spiritual healing are woven together so closely that it is impossible to distinguish clearly between them.

Spiritual healing involves, first of all, the forgiveness of sins:

> You are compassionate, O Ineffable One; by your invisible hand, O God who loves mankind, you have sealed our senses with your divine oil. Look down from heaven upon him (her) who appeals to you in faith and asks for the forgiveness of

his(her) sins. Grant healing of both soul and body, so that he (she) may glorify you and magnify your power.[25]

You are without beginning, eternal, Holy of Holies, who sent down your only-begotten Son to heal every disease and every infirmity of our souls and bodies: send down your Holy Spirit and sanctify this oil; and grant that it may bring full pardon from sin to your servant (name) who is to be anointed, and the inheritance of the kingdom of Heaven.[26]

Forgiveness of sins is so central to the rite that, since approximately the thirteenth century, a prayer of absolution, adapted from the rite of confession, was added to the rite of anointing just before the dismissal. From roughly the same time,[27] but especially since the seventeenth century, under the influence of Metropolitan Peter Moghila of Kiev,[28] Slavic and some other Orthodox churches have required persons desiring to be anointed first to undergo the sacrament of confession.[29] This latter development is unfortunate, inasmuch as, under the influence of scholasticism, it tends to separate the mysteries of healing and forgiveness too sharply. A central theme in the rite of anointing is precisely the fact that healing and forgiveness are intimately connected and cannot be separated—forgiveness is mediated through the prayers and the anointing with oil in the rite.

[25]Troparion at the Praises.

[26]Prayer of the priest at the first anointing.

[27]Cf *Sinai gr. 973*, described in the previous chapter.

[28]Peter Moghila, *Trebnik* (Kiev, 1646), 446. Peter instructs priests to hear the sick person's confession prior to performing the anointing, and then to commune him/her immediately following the anointing.

[29]See, for example, the recent *Pastoral Guide to the Holy Mysteries* (Cambridge: British Antiochian Orthodox Deanery, 2001), 90, #149.2, an English translation of a guide published in Arabic by the Patriarchate of Antioch in 1996.

Spiritual healing, moreover, must be understood positively, and it cannot be reduced simply to the removal of passions and forgiveness of sin, important as these are. Its goal is eminently positive:

For you are a great and wonderful God: you keep your covenant and your mercy toward those who love you, granting forgiveness of sins through your holy Child, Jesus Christ, who grants us a new birth from sin, who gives light to the blind, who raises up those who are cast down, who loves the righteous and shows mercy to sinners, who leads us out of darkness and the shadow of death, saying to those in chains, "Go forth," and to those who sit in darkness, "Open your eyes." You made the light of the knowledge of his countenance to shine in our hearts when for our sakes he revealed himself upon earth and dwelt among us. To those who accepted him, he gave the power to become children of God, granting us adoption through the washing of regeneration and removing us from the tyranny of the devil. For it did not please you that we should be cleansed by blood, but by holy oil, so you gave us the image of his cross, that we might become the flock of Christ, a royal priesthood, a holy nation; and you purified us with water and sanctified us with the Holy Spirit. . . . Let this oil, O Lord, become the oil of gladness, the oil of sanctification, a royal robe, an armor of might, the averting of every work of the devil, an unassailable seal, the joy of the heart, and eternal rejoicing. Grant that those who are anointed with this oil of regeneration may be fearsome to their adversaries, and that they may shine with the radiance of your saints, having neither stain nor defect, and that they may attain your everlasting rest and receive the prize of their high calling.[30]

[30]Prayer of the first priest.

Here we see spelled out the positive aspects of spiritual healing, which hearken back to the grace we received at our baptism. Anointing of the sick, just like baptism, is not only for the forgiveness of sins, but for new birth, for enlightenment, for liberation from slavery, for adoption into sonship. The oil we are now using reminds us of the oil of gladness with which we were anointed prior to baptism, as well as the anointing with chrism we received immediately after we emerged from the font. We are thus reminded of the task that was set before us at our baptism: to "shine with the radiance of the saints." Now, as we face the possibility of our death, we pray that we may attain everlasting rest and receive the prize of our high calling. Here, as we come face to face with the enemy, we are reminded in no uncertain terms about the victory that was guaranteed us in our baptism. Deliberately and consciously, the Church now brings us back to that starting point when each of us "put on Christ,"[31] received the Holy Spirit, and became a member of the royal priesthood. As we approach the conclusion of the race, we are reminded of the goal that lies ahead, which is nothing less than the ultimate victory promised by Christ.

Thus the healing implied by this rite is more than forgiveness of sins and the restoration of physical, emotional, and spiritual health. It is rather a cosmic event, in which all things are set back into their proper perspective. Sin, sickness, and death are conquered, made powerless through the operation of Christ and the Holy Spirit. Our defeat is transformed into victory as our suffering is joined to the suffering and victory of Christ on the cross. The dramatic effects of baptism, so central in the life of Christians, are, in a sense, brought back to the forefront of conscious-

[31]Gal 3.27.

ness as the Church gathers around its members who now each face their own cross.

Holistic Healing

From what has been stated thus far, it is evident that the rites of healing are holistic. Anointing of the sick addresses not just the body, but the soul and the spirit as well. And it does so in the broader context in which persons facing illness find themselves.

First, the rite makes clear that illness, whether physical or mental, needs to be seen as part of a larger whole, as one of several consequences and manifestations of the fall. With the fall of Adam, both humanity and the entire cosmos were affected. Illness, therefore, is not the root problem, but only a symptom. The far more significant consequence of the fall was the rupture of the communion between God and humanity, between humans among themselves, and between humanity and the rest of creation. For Christians, sickness and death are not the real problem: rather, it is alienation from God, and the resulting spiritual death, which are the real tragedy.

This is precisely where modern medicine often falls short. Medical doctors seek to heal and restore the body without concern for the spiritual dimensions of human existence. The mental health profession, which deals with the psyche, similarly ignores this deeper truth about human existence—either seeing mental disorders merely as the result of some chemical imbalance, and thus treating them with psychotropic medications; or, depending on their own understanding of the human person, treating patients with no regard for the Christian understanding that healthy human existence is nothing less than life in communion with God and others.[32] This does not mean that the modern medical establishment is of no use, or that Christians should not avail themselves of what it offers. It simply means that modern medicine does not address the total reality of human existence, and does not therefore offer a healing that is ultimate in nature.

The Church's understanding of health thus differs from that of the medical profession. The healing that the health professions can offer is only temporary in nature, while the Church offers healing that is not bound by this world, by space or time. In fact, the entire mission of the Church, from our birth to our funeral and beyond, is to bring us true healing—reconciliation between God and humanity, true life in the kingdom—as we saw in the first chapter. The anointing of the sick, made available to the person facing serious illness, is but one small part of the overall work of the Church. Yet, even in this particular ministry, healing is offered within that broader, more comprehensive framework.

How, then, does the rite accomplish this healing? How does it address the isolation which is the inevitable consequence of illness? How does it restore purpose to a life which no longer seems to have any useful purpose?

First, the anointing of the sick, performed *in church* (when possible) and *by the Church* (with the participation of both clergy and church members expressing the presence of the Church), aims precisely at reintegrating the sick person into the community (the Church). Either the sick person is brought into the church, or the Church comes to where the sick person may be. In either case,

---

[32]This is not to say, of course, that there are no mental health professionals who consciously adopt a more Christian approach. In North America, there is an active Orthodox Christian Association of Medicine, Psychology, and Religion, which holds annual meetings and conferences. See *www.ocampr.org.*

the Church as community stands with the sick in their time of suffering, reintegrating them into the body of Christ. This is one reason the rite is so long—at one time taking up an entire week, and now at least several hours. The rite breaks through the isolation, for Christ and the Church stand with the sick person at this critical juncture of life—one which every person must face one day!

This ecclesial dimension of the rite is central, and it is already evident in James 5: When a person is sick, all the elders are to come to him. This emphasizes the point that the *whole Church* is to gather around its sick members. Subsequently, as the rite develops, it is done *in church*, at one time in a *eucharistic* context, and requires the presence of seven presbyters, a number expressing fullness. Thus the entire Church participates in this sacrament, as, indeed, in all the sacraments.

The whole Church should be involved in this rite of healing because the sickness of an individual, just like the sin of any member, affects the entire Church. The whole body suffers when one of its members falls ill or sins.[33] This also helps to explain why, in earlier forms of the rite, rubrics indicate that all those in attendance are to be anointed, and not just the sick person.[34] It is precisely this sense of community which is so often missing in parish life. This is one symptom of the crisis which affects our modern society and the modern parish: we tend to see ourselves as *individuals* who come to church to satisfy our individual needs, and we have little contact with our neighbor standing next to us. Thus, when a member of our parish falls ill or ceases to come, we hardly notice. Symptomatic, too, is the fact that this sacrament

[33]Cf. 1 Cor 12.26.

[34]As is still done in those parishes that celebrate the service of anointing on Wednesday of Holy Week.

has generally fallen into disuse,[35] or, more commonly, has become a private ceremony, most often performed in the isolation of a hospital room, with only the parish priest and perhaps a family member in attendance.

Second, the rite reestablishes a future, for in Christ there is no death. Sickness and death are no longer a prison, but a threshold to new life. As Fr Alexander Schmemann puts it so well,

> Healing is a sacrament because its purpose or end is not health as such, but the *entrance* of man into the life of the Kingdom, into the "joy and peace" of the Holy Spirit. In Christ, everything in this world, and this means health and disease, joy and suffering, has become an ascension to, and entrance into this new life, its experience and anticipation.[36]

This theme is brought out in a striking way in the prayer of the first priest, as we have already seen above. The prayer begins by recounting what Christ has accomplished on our behalf by granting us forgiveness, new birth, and enlightenment. The prayer then concludes:

> Let this oil, O Lord, become the oil of gladness, the oil of sanctification, a royal robe, an armor of might, the averting of every work of the devil, an unassailable seal, the joy of the heart, and eternal rejoicing. Grant that those who are

---

[35]There are several reasons for this: 1) Since the seventeenth century in Russia, under the westernizing influence of Metropolitan Peter Moghila of Kiev (+1646), the sacrament has been understood as "extreme unction," i.e., a sacrament for the dying; 2) The difficulty of finding seven presbyters to perform the rite, as well as its sheer length, made it cumbersome to perform, at least in parishes.

[36]A. Schmemann, *For the Life of the World: Sacraments and Orthodoxy* (Crestwood, NY: SVS Press, 1973), 102–103.

---

anointed with this oil of regeneration may be fearsome to their adversaries, and that they may shine with the radiance of your saints, having neither stain nor defect, and that they may attain your everlasting rest and receive the prize of their high calling.[37]

Thus, whether the patients recover or die—both possibilities are implied here—they are brought back into the reality they entered at their baptism: the victory over sin and death. Indeed, the prayer recalls the themes that were prominent in baptism, the pre-baptismal anointing with the oil of gladness,[38] as well as the anointing with chrism immediately following baptism. Their future, whether they live or die, is assured, for in Christ there is no death.

[37]Prayer of the first priest.

[38]The prayer for the blessing of the pre-baptismal oil seems itself to be derived from a healing prayer: "O Lord and Master, the God of our fathers, who sent unto those who were in the ark of Noah your dove, bearing in its beak a twig of olive, the token of reconciliation and salvation from the flood, the foreshadowing of the mystery of grace, and who provided the fruit of the olive for the fulfilling of your holy mysteries, who thereby fill them that were under the Law with your Holy Spirit, and perfect them that are under grace. Bless also this holy oil with the power and operation and indwelling of your Holy Spirit, that it may be an anointing unto incorruption, an armor of righteousness, to the renewing of soul and body, to the averting of every assault of the devil, to deliverance from all evil of those who shall be anointed with it in faith, or who partake* thereof, unto your glory and the glory of your only-begotten Son, and of your all-holy and good and life-creating Spirit, now and ever, and unto ages of ages."

*Literally: "eat." Since there is no evidence that people ever consumed the oil used for pre-baptismal anointing, it stands to reason that this prayer originates in a different context, similar to other early prayers for the blessing of healing oil in sources such as the fourth-century *Prayer Book of Serapion*.

Not only is their future assured, but their life now has a purpose. Their suffering is joined to the cross. The suffering thus becomes a *martyria*, which is a *contribution to the life of the community*, for the way in which we suffer and die says more about our Christian faith than any other words or deeds. The anointing once more identifies the suffering individual with Christ as king, priest, and prophet, just as does the anointing administered at baptism. This is the ultimate healing at which the sacrament aims. If physical healing is granted, and indeed it is prayed for, it is, of course, accepted with gratitude. But this is not the primary aim of the rite: all those who are healed will ultimately get sick again and die, just as those whom Jesus healed or even raised from the dead also eventually died. The goal of healing is the restoration of fallen, sickly, and mortal humanity into communion with Christ, and with the Church, which is already the manifestation of the kingdom on earth.

CHAPTER 4

What Can Be Done?
Some Pastoral Suggestions

The rite of anointing of the sick, as it has developed over the centuries, is a wonderfully rich expression of the Church's care for its members. It is, however, only part of an entire complex of rites which shepherd Christians through the key moments of life, from birth to death and beyond. It is therefore important to consider the rite not in isolation, but as a part of a lifelong process. When we are born, we are greeted with prayer on the first day after birth,[1] on the eighth day after birth,[2] and at the churching on the fortieth day.[3] At some point later, we are baptized and chrismated, after which we participate regularly in the liturgical and eucharistic life of the Church. The Church then blesses our marriage as we take that significant step in our lives. In each of these, as well as in the daily cycle of vespers and matins, the Church prays for our health, both physical and spiritual. As we approach the end of our earthly life, the Church is there at the "Office of the Parting of the Soul from the Body."[4]

[1]Cf. I.F. Hapgood, trans., *Service Book of the Holy Orthodox-Catholic Apostolic Church* (New York: Association Press, 1922) (reprinted multiple times by the Antiochian Orthodox Christian Diocese), 266–7.

[2]"Prayers at the Naming of a Child," ibid., 267.

[3]Ibid., 268–70.

[4]Ibid., 360–67.

After we die, the Church accompanies us to our grave, where we lie awaiting the second coming and the universal resurrection.[5] When we fall seriously ill, the Church is there with the anointing of the sick.

The form in which the anointing of the sick takes place, however, varies greatly from parish to parish. At times, the priest alone comes to the hospital or to the home of an ill parishioner and performs an abbreviated form of the rite. Occasionally, the sick person is brought to the church for the celebration, and a few other parishioners may be in attendance. Particularly in churches following Slavic traditions, the rite is rarely performed, because it is understood to be a rite for the dying, the "last rites." Consequently, both patients and their families misunderstand its purpose and see it rather as a last resort, a capitulation to imminent death. The priest who comes is perceived more as a "grim reaper" than as a "physician of souls and bodies."

Most commonly, however, parishioners experience the service on the evening of Holy Wednesday—and this service is typically the most popular and best-attended service during Holy Week. The vast majority of Orthodox have witnessed the rite of anointing the sick only in this way, and are little aware of the rite's original purpose and context. When performed in this way, the rite is understood to be a preparation for the reception of communion on Holy Thursday and Pascha, and often a substitute for the sacrament of confession.

In both practices described above, the meaning of the rite of anointing is not fully evident. In the pages that follow, then, I make several proposals for a fuller use of this important sacramental act.

[5]Ibid., 368–434. There are separate funeral rites for the laity, for priests, and for young children.

Restoring the Ministry of Healing in the Parish

The Church's ministry of healing is not the responsibility of the priest alone, but needs to be shared by other members of the parish.

> Is any among you sick? Let him call for the elders of the church, and let them pray over him, anointing him with oil in the name of the Lord; and the prayer of faith will save the sick man, and the Lord will raise him up; and if he has committed sins, he will be forgiven. Therefore confess your sins to one another, and pray for one another, that you may be healed. (Jas 5.13–16)

A careful reading of this key scriptural passage referring to healing, as well as Mark 6.7–13, reveals first of all that this ministry of healing is given to the Church precisely as the Church. This is why the "elders" (note the plural) are to be called when one of the members falls ill. It is the responsibility of the entire Church, the entire body, to care for its ailing members. When one suffers, the whole body suffers, as St Paul reminds us in 1 Corinthians 12.26. The "elders" or presbyters mentioned in the above passage are not priests in the modern sense of the word, but precisely the leaders, the representatives of the local, eucharistic community of Christians. Nor is this ministry only the task of the pastor,[6] the one who presides over the local church. James stresses precisely the role of the entire community, which is called to rally around its ailing members to pray over them and to anoint them.

[6]In the early Church, this would have been the bishop. In later centuries, as bishops became the rulers of territorial dioceses, the function of presiding over a local community (the parish) was increasingly assumed by presbyters (priests).

This communal character of the sacrament of healing is expressed through the later rule requiring that multiple (ideally, seven) presbyters be present.

An unfortunate consequence of this requirement for numerous presbyters has been the greatly decreased frequency in the celebration of the sacrament, due to the difficulty in gathering together seven priests. This may be one reason the rite came to be celebrated once a year, and usually only in cathedrals. Needless to say, it is a rare occasion indeed when the rite can be celebrated with a full complement of seven priests.

The main point behind the requirement that there be seven priests, however, is precisely that the fullness of the Church should be present to minister to the sick, for the number seven is a symbol of fullness and completeness. Furthermore, as we have just seen, the "presbyters" mentioned in the above passage from the Epistle of James are not like our modern-day parish priests. During the first few centuries, each local eucharistic community was headed by a bishop, who presided at liturgical celebrations and, with the help of deacons, administered church affairs. Advising the bishop was a council of elders, the "presbyters."[7] The presbyters, therefore, were more like members of modern-day parish councils. They were elected or chosen on the basis of their spiritual maturity and their witness to the faith in times of persecution, just as today we elect persons to parish councils on the basis of their evident maturity of faith and their wisdom.

Transposing this model to the present day, it is evident that the responsibility for ministering to the sick falls not just on the parish priest, but on the lay members of the parish as well, particularly those who hold responsible positions. It could, therefore,

---

[7]The word "presbyter" comes from the Greek word meaning "elder."

well be a job requirement for all members of the parish council to engage in this activity. As the elders in the community, parish council members are expected not just to administer the parish's finances, but to be models of Christian life. Indeed, all Christians are charged with the ministry of visiting the sick, and all will be held accountable for this at the Last Judgment. If we do this, we will hear the words of Christ:

> Come, O blessed of my Father, inherit the kingdom prepared for you from the foundation of the world; for I was hungry and you gave me food, I was thirsty and you gave me drink, I was a stranger and you welcomed me, I was naked and you clothed me, I was sick and you visited me, I was in prison and you came to me. . . . Truly I say to you, as you did it to one of the least of these my brethren, you did it to me. (Matt 25.34–6, 40)

In too many parishes the ministry to the sick is relegated to the priest. Indeed, the priest does have a responsibility in this regard, and his presence is required for the celebration of the sacrament of anointing. However, it cannot be his responsibility alone, and there is a great deal that all the members of the parish can do. They can and must visit the sick—first of all sick members of the parish community, but then also anyone else they know. They do this because in the other they see the face of Christ. They do this because, by doing so, they bring the presence and the message of Christ to their neighbors in the Church and in the world at large. In this way, they help to spread the gospel message to the world in which they live, and thus exercise their own priestly ministry, given to them at baptism.

Pastors must therefore do their best to engage all the laity in this important ministry. They can involve parishioners in visiting the sick and shut-ins. They can develop and train interested individuals in the skills needed for this task. They should mention the names of sick persons at appropriate points in the liturgical services, including at litanies, at intercessions during the Great Entrance, and in the conclusion of the eucharistic prayer.[8] They can involve young persons in holding liturgies in nursing homes. In each city, clergy could work together to develop "Saints Cosmas and Damian Societies"[9] to carry out this ministry, as well as to organize celebrations of the eucharistic liturgies in long-term care facilities and nursing homes.

Finally, pastors ought to bring back into practice the service of anointing of the sick as a properly liturgical celebration, normally performed in church, and with as many of the faithful in attendance as possible. Where possible, ill parishioners should be brought to the church, and the rite can be celebrated over several people at a time. In this way, the sick can be reintegrated into the life of the Church, surrounded by family, friends, and the members of Christ's body. All will pray for and with the sick as the priest or priests in attendance repeatedly lay their hands on them and anoint them—just as they laid hands on them and anointed them when they were first received into the Church at their baptism. In both cases, the event is profoundly ecclesial, as the entire Church is involved both in receiving new members into the Church at baptism,[10] and now standing in solidarity and

[8]The whole concluding section of the anaphora in the liturgies of both John Chrysostom and Basil the Great consists of intercessory prayer, in which names of individuals are mentioned.

[9]Named after the two best-known "unmercenary saints" and physicians.

[10]It is obvious that baptism is itself a profoundly ecclesial rite, and thus baptisms too should be performed in the presence of the entire community when possible. Fr Alexander Schmemann has argued this forcefully in his

ministering to its ailing members at this critical juncture in their lives.

In this way, the meaning and implications of the rite become more fully evident, both to the sick persons being anointed and to the parish community. Parishioners express their love, care, and concern for one or more of their members. Together with the priests, they bring and proclaim the gospel message of forgiveness and healing, thus sharing in Christ's own priesthood and ministry. As for the sick who are the recipients of this rite, they are provided the opportunity themselves to be martyrs, witnesses before the entire community that suffering leads ultimately to the victory of the cross. They are reconciled with God and with the body of Christ, the Church, and the real meaning and dignity of their life as Christians is reaffirmed.

There are, of course, times when it is not possible to conduct the rite in the church. When it is not possible to bring the sick to the church, then the church should go to where the sick person is, to the home, the hospital, or the long-term care facility. In ancient times in the Byzantine Empire, monasteries were the first hospitals, so the ecclesial context was evident. The eleventh-century rite described in chapter two called for the celebration of the rite in a domestic church—at a time when many homes in cities such as Constantinople did contain such chapels. In modern times, this is no longer the case: not only are there no domestic chapels, but the sick are not kept at home. Those seriously ill are typically sent to hospitals, nursing homes, or long-term care—and in this way they are isolated from both church and society. It thus becomes all the more important for the Church to gather wherever the sick may be, to break through the isolation that inevitably results.

classic work on the subject, *Of Water and the Spirit.*

In most cases today, the priest goes to visit the sick alone. He prays with them, he hears their confessions, anoints them, and brings them communion. He does this precisely as the representative of the Church, and in this way what he does certainly is ecclesial. Nevertheless, even if he may represent the Church, the priest is not the totality of the whole priestly community, and something is lacking when no other members of the Church are present. We sense this intuitively at other significant events in our lives—birthdays, weddings, graduations, etc. How sad and diminished these events would be if no one else were present to celebrate with us! Christian life, in particular, is essentially communal: the Greek word for church, *ecclesia*, means "the assembly," and the Church has from the very beginning stressed the importance of gathering together frequently.

Thus, if the rite must be celebrated elsewhere than in the church, the priest should strive to bring parishioners with him. If the model in the Epistle of James is followed, these would include the elders of the community, members of the parish council. Often, parishes also have (or should have) organizations with the particular task of ministering to the sick and the elderly. They visit them, bring them to church on Sundays, help with funeral arrangements, and prepare mercy meals. Having the members of such groups accompany the clergy for the rite of anointing would be a natural extension of the ministry they are already performing, and would give this ministry an important liturgical dimension.

The General Anointing on Holy Wednesday

In Greek practice, followed also by Antiochian parishes, the rite of anointing of the sick is celebrated on the evening of Holy

Wednesday. In most cases, this service replaces the regular service appointed for that time, the matins of Holy Thursday.[11] This general anointing service has arguably become the most popular service of Holy Week, even though neither the *Typikon of St Sabas*, followed by the Slavic churches, nor the nineteenth-century *Typikon of the Great Church*, followed by Greek and Antiochian churches, even mentions it. This is a clear example of the triumph of popular piety, which in the latter tradition has placed the rite in such a prominent position. So popular has the rite become that many parishioners from parishes following Slavic practice will go to a parish that does celebrate the Holy Wednesday anointing, and there is a resulting pressure on the former to introduce the practice.

However, as Fr Koumarianos has pointed out, this practice is not without its problems. First, the matins of Holy Thursday has an important place in the liturgical structure of Holy Week, as it contains a rich hymnography connected with the celebration of the Last Supper, the betrayal of Christ by Judas, and the events leading up to the passion.[12] Eliminating this service leaves an important gap in Holy Week.

Furthermore, even if the matins service is not replaced, celebrating the rite of anointing at this point interrupts the liturgical flow of Holy Week by drawing the attention of the faithful away

[11]In contemporary Orthodox practice, the services of Holy Week are celebrated one half day in anticipation. Thus, the matins service appointed in the *Typikon* for Holy Thursday morning is celebrated on Wednesday evening. On the problems and confusion caused by this practice, see the article by Fr Pavlos Koumarianos, "Liturgical Problems of Holy Week," *SVTQ* 46 (2002): 3–21, especially 15–16.

[12]For an English translation of the hymns of Holy Thursday, see Mother Mary and Kallistos Ware, trans., *The Lenten Triodion* (London and Boston: Faber and Faber, 1978), 548–57.

from the events surrounding the passion of Christ, and back onto themselves. The genius of the liturgical structure of the paschal cycle consists in its devoting six entire weeks to our preparation for Pascha. During these six weeks of Great Lent, we fast, we confess our sins, we lead a more intense spiritual life. Then, beginning with Lazarus Saturday and Palm Sunday, we shift our attention to Christ's passion.[13] The hymns of Holy Week turn our attention away from ourselves and focus it instead on the dramatic events of salvation. Through a complete cycle of services, the Church now accompanies Christ at this critical moment in the history of salvation. Celebrating the service of anointing on Holy Wednesday completely disrupts this flow.

An unintended and unfortunate consequence of the Holy Wednesday anointing is that, for many of the faithful, this service marks the beginning of the liturgical celebration of Holy Week. Some parishes do not even celebrate the bridegroom services[14] or the presanctified liturgies[15] appointed for the first three days of the week, and the anointing service, which is not even prescribed in the *Typikon*, begins the Holy Week cycle.

In those parishes that do celebrate the service of anointing on Holy Wednesday, it would therefore be preferable to shift the celebration to a time before Holy Week, perhaps to a day during the sixth week of Lent. It could then serve as a final preparation for our entrance into the week of the passion. The same could be

[13]Cf. A. Schmemann, *Great Lent*.

[14]These are the services of matins (*orthros*) of Holy Monday, Tuesday, and Wednesday, whose theme of eschatological watchfulness is encapsulated by the troparion, "Behold, the bridegroom comes at midnight . . ."

[15]Presanctified liturgies, appointed for Wednesdays and Fridays during Lent, as well as Monday through Wednesday of Holy Week, are vespers services that conclude with the distribution of the eucharist, which has been consecrated at the liturgy of the previous Sunday.

done in those parishes of Slavic heritage that do not presently have this practice, though care should be taken to avoid additional pitfalls, discussed below, inherent in this general anointing.

In those churches that celebrate this general anointing, the rite has also come to serve as a substitute for the sacrament of confession. This understanding has become so entrenched that the sacrament of anointing is no longer understood to be a rite for the physical and spiritual healing of gravely ill persons—a meaning that is easily discerned in the text of the service. Rather, it is interpreted as a generic rite of healing, with no connection to any particular, serious illness. The Holy Wednesday rite is typically explained as, "We are all sick, and we all need healing!" But such an understanding leads to an almost complete loss of the rite's real purpose. In this new context, the distinction between the sacraments of anointing of the sick and confession (which is precisely for spiritual healing and reconciliation) is also blurred, and this gives parishioners an excuse to avoid the rite of confession altogether. Furthermore, in Orthodox tradition it is precisely the regular participation in the sacrament of communion which is "for the healing of soul and body," as the formula for the reception of communion itself states.

Ultimately, we can only conclude that this general anointing on Holy Wednesday dilutes the original focus and purpose of the rite. Instead of specifically addressing persons facing the challenge of serious illness, it is now used for a different purpose altogether. While it is obviously not possible to abolish this Holy Wednesday practice, care should at least be taken to ensure that it not be abused, and that there should be occasions for the proper celebration of the service over those parishioners who do face serious illness, and who therefore benefit from it the most.

Anointing and Confession

Evidently, the rites of confession and anointing of the sick are closely related. Both clearly address our fallen condition and provide a remedy. But they are not the same, and to use one as a substitute for the other is to misunderstand them both. The sacrament of confession addresses the reality that we all sin after baptism and provides a means for reconciliation. The anointing of the sick, while it does address the forgiveness of sins, focuses also on the reality of physical and mental suffering, and it should not be used as a substitute for sacramental confession.

At the same time, in churches following Slavic practice, it has become customary to require persons over whom the rite is celebrated first to confess their sins, and the same seems to have been true at one time in the Greek tradition.[16] S.V. Bulgakov's classical handbook for clergy of the Russian Orthodox Church, for example, states: "The sick person receiving the sacrament [of anointing] must be prepared for its reception by confession."[17] Aware of the fact that this has not always been the case, Bulgakov indicates that this is not an absolute requirement, since the rite of anointing itself includes the forgiveness of sins.[18] K. Nikolskii, however, is even more definite in requiring confession and does not allow for any exception.[19] This development, due largely to the influence of Peter Moghila in the seventeenth century, also diminishes the value of the rite of anointing itself, which closely

[16]See the rite in the twelfth-century *Sinai gr. 973,* described in chapter two.

[17]S.V. Bulgakov, *Nastol'naia Kniga* (Kharkov', 1900), 1182.

[18]Ibid., 1182, n 3.

[19]K. Nikolskii, *Posobie k izucheniiu ustava bogosluzheniia pravoslavnoi tserkvi* (St Petersburg, 1900), 733.

links healing and forgiveness, both being mediated through the anointing with oil.

It should also be noted that, in both the Greek and the Slavic traditions, the sacrament of anointing may be administered only to persons in communion with the Church, which presupposes that these persons are active participants in the sacramental life of the Church—a participation that normally includes both regular confession and frequent communion. For such persons, then, logic would indicate that sacramental confession should not be an absolute prerequisite immediately before the anointing service.

Anointing and Eucharist

The practice of receiving communion in conjunction with the anointing of the sick is ancient. In the Byzantine tradition, as we have seen, this rite was at one time celebrated as part of seven eucharistic liturgies on seven consecutive days. It is quite likely that the excessive length of the services, as well as the gradual decline in the frequency of communion, led to the separation of the two. Yet it clearly remained the practice that persons receiving anointing also received communion, either just before or just following the rite. Possibly, the requirement for confession prior to the anointing may originally have been connected not to the anointing, but to preparation for the reception of communion. This would have happened because, with the gradual decline in the frequency of communion over the centuries, it became customary, particularly in the Slavic traditions, to require confession before each communion.[20] It is not surprising, therefore, that it is

[20] On this development, see for example Erickson, "Penitential Discipline in the Orthodox Canonical Tradition."

precisely in the Slavic tradition that we find the legalistic requirement for sacramental confession prior to the anointing.

For the Orthodox, reception of the eucharist is the deepest and fullest expression of one's membership in the Church. It is also the greatest sign of reconciliation both with God and with each other. It is the ultimate goal of the sacraments of baptism and chrismation, in which the newly baptized are grafted into Christ's body, the Church. It is the goal of the sacrament of confession, which reconciles us when we fall into sin and restores us into the communion of the Church. It only stands to reason, therefore, that the anointing of the sick, which also grants healing, forgiveness, and restoration, should also culminate in the reception of the eucharist.

Several solutions are possible. The rite of anointing could simply be combined with the eucharistic liturgy, as was once the case. Given the fact, however, that the anointing is typically celebrated either at a home or a hospital, with few people in attendance, it is preferable simply to commune the sick individual from the reserved sacrament. If, however, the anointing of the sick is performed in the church with large numbers in attendance, then it might indeed be possible to unite it to a full eucharistic celebration. This would, however, have the effect of greatly lengthening what is already a long service. Thus, this option would likely work only in those cathedrals or monasteries where the Eucharist is already celebrated daily, and where the rite could easily be incorporated along the lines found in the eleventh-century manuscript[21] described in chapter two. Any such action would require further discussion and the approval of the local bishop.

[21]Paris manuscript *Coislin 213.*

Celebrating the Rite

The full text of the rite of anointing is provided in Appendix One. The rite is quite long, and an abbreviated rite, adapted from a fourteenth–fifteenth-century Slavic manuscript, is provided in Appendix Two.

The full rite calls for seven priests, but, as we have already seen, this reflects the fully ecclesial character of the rite and should not be taken in a literal or legalistic fashion. Behind this requirement lies the point that it is the fullness of the Church that gathers around the sick person. Clergy who are asked to celebrate the rite, therefore, need not try to get seven priests together (a practical impossibility in most cases), and should instead seek to involve their parishioners to the greatest extent possible. In particular, they should encourage the "elders of the church," in the words of James 5, to participate. In the modern situation, this could well include members of the parish council, as well as others who actively participate in the parish's outreach programs.

The length of the anointing service may, to some, be an obstacle. Yet the very length of the rite provides an important testimony to the Church's care for her members. At this difficult moment in the life of Christians, the Church takes the time and the effort to be with them, to pray with and for them, to anoint them, to bring to them the gospel message of love and forgiveness. An important aspect of the ethos of Orthodox liturgical worship is that services are not rushed. Even the regular Sunday liturgy typically takes an hour and a half or more! Offering praise and intercessory prayer to God, listening to the proclamation of God's word—these deserve serious time and effort on the part of Christians. How much more is this so when one of the Church's members comes face to face with severe illness, with the possibility of death itself?

There will, of course, be times when it is not practical to celebrate the rite in its entirety. Particularly when a priest visits the sick in a hospital setting, it is common to celebrate it in abbreviated form, such as that presented in Appendix Two. While this shortened rite does contain the essential components of the full version, it is obviously much less comprehensive and should be used only at those times when the full rite cannot be performed.

In current practice, as we have seen, the sacrament of anointing of the sick is celebrated rarely. The reasons for this are complex, but include the length and complexity of the service, the requirement for having seven priests, as well as the erroneous perception of the rite as "extreme unction" in some traditions. This is a situation that ought to be corrected, first of all through preaching and instruction, and secondly by more regular and frequent celebration of the rite.

Nothing would prevent, for example, a parish from scheduling a service of anointing on an annual, or even quarterly, basis. Parishioners could be marshaled to bring ailing and shut-in parishioners to the church for the occasion. Given current demographics, most Orthodox parishes have numerous elderly and ailing members. In larger metropolitan areas with multiple parishes, these services could be done on a deanery level, with the location rotating among the various churches. This would give clergy the opportunity to concelebrate and to build a sense of unity among both clergy and faithful in a given area. It would also make parishioners aware of the many afflicted persons in their midst, persons who otherwise simply fade away unnoticed.

At these services, sick persons should be anointed first, as the rite focuses primarily on them. But it would also be appropriate for all the faithful in attendance at these services to be anointed as well—as we have seen was the case in Byzantine practice during the medieval period. This is justified, as we have seen, by the fact that the sickness of an individual, physical as well as mental and spiritual, affects those around him or her—the immediate family as well as the parish community. Further, the message of healing, forgiveness, and reconciliation in the rite is addressed equally to the entire assembly.

Perhaps this practice could even replace the Holy Wednesday anointing service described above. Done at some point before Holy Week, it would restore the proper focus of the rite on the seriously ill, while involving the entire parish family in this critical ministry. What better Lenten effort and preparation for the celebration of the Lord's passion than our own participation in the healing ministry inaugurated by Christ and handed down to his disciples and to the Church! By participating in the rite of anointing, the faithful become both the recipients of this healing ministry, as well as the agents through whom it is given to the Church.

Finally, it should be noted that the sacrament of anointing, like, indeed, all the sacraments, is restricted to baptized Orthodox Christians. This is because participation in the sacramental, liturgical life of the Church implies a full commitment to the one, holy, catholic, and apostolic Church and to the faith which it proclaims through the centuries. Participation in the sacraments, from the very beginning, was restricted to those who were members of the Church, as we can see, for example, in the most ancient church order, which dates to the late first or early second century: "No one is to eat or drink of your eucharist except those baptized in the name of the Lord."[22] The same restriction applies to all the sacraments, including the sacramental anointing of the sick.

---

[22]*Didache* 9.

While this restriction may seem unduly harsh in our present day, it simply reflects the ecclesial dimensions of this rite, as of all the sacraments in general. The sacrament of healing has as its goal the reintegration of the sick into the fullness of the life of the Church, and the rite would be completely meaningless for someone who does not desire this.

What about Ministry to Non-Orthodox?

Does this mean, however, that the Church's ministry to the sick does not or cannot extend beyond the canonical limits of the Church? The answer, of course, is a clear no.

Christ came to bring healing to the whole world, and not just to a particular, select group. And the Church's task is precisely to carry out in the world the task inaugurated by Christ. This ministry is carried out within the Church in its sacramental and liturgical life. But in the world, this task is carried out by all the faithful, the laity, the people of God.[23] When we are baptized, when we "put on Christ,"[24] we become the presence of Christ in the world, charged with continuing Christ's ministry to the world in which we live—our homes, our places of work, our society. This involves spreading the gospel, "the good news," wherever we happen to be. And we do this not merely through words but, more importantly, by our lives, by our care for the poor and needy of this world, by our ministry to the sick whenever and wherever they might be.

---

[23]The word laity derives from the Greek expression, *laos tou Theou*, the "people of God," an expression used in Scripture to refer to the Church.
[24]Cf. Gal 3.27.

Though this ministry of the faithful does not take a liturgical form, it is no less significant. We Christians are charged with bringing the healing, reconciliation, and forgiveness that we receive through the sacramental life of the Church to the world in which we live. When we gather for the eucharistic liturgy each Sunday, we pray and intercede for the whole world, "on behalf of all and for all," Christian and non-Christian alike. When we give alms to the poor or visit the sick, we do not ask whether or not they are Orthodox. We are called to help them because they too are made in the image and likeness of God, they too are to us the face of Christ. This is clear in the text from Matthew quoted earlier, which concludes with these words:

> "Lord, when did we see thee hungry or thirsty or a stranger or naked or sick or in prison, and did not minister to thee?" Then he will answer them, "Truly I say to you, as you did it not to one of the least of these, you did it not to me." And they will go away into eternal punishment, but the righteous into eternal life. (Matt 25.44–6)

Clearly, ministry to others, to the neighbor, whoever she or he may be, is a Christian imperative, for which we will all be held accountable.

What then, can Orthodox Christians do in ministering to the sick beyond the narrow confines of their parish? Certainly they can visit with them and provide necessary assistance. In doing this, they are simply extending God's own love for humanity, because God never desires our suffering. They can pray for the sick and even, if the sick person is willing, lay hands on them and anoint them with oil taken, for example, from a lamp burning before the icon of one of the unmercenary healing saints. They can listen to the sick and simply be with them in their time of trouble—often without even the need to say anything. In doing this, they are no different from their parish priest who, while visiting his ailing parishioners in a hospital or institution, also encounters and ministers to any others he happens to run into, whether in the neighboring bed, in the hallway, or out on the street.

In doing this, Orthodox Christians are exercising their priestly ministry and are bringing the presence of the Church, of Christ himself, out into the world. This is an area in which Orthodox witness in modern western society has been generally weak. Orthodox communities are often content to live in their small, at times narrowly ethnic, enclaves. They are not comfortable with outreach to the wider community—whether through social welfare programs such as soup kitchens, prison ministry, or ministry to the sick and elderly. Yet these are effective means of spreading the gospel, the good news that Christ offers the world through the Church.

Such ministry is, of course, not liturgical in the proper sense of the word. Yet it flows out of the liturgy, for it is putting the words we utter in the liturgy into action. If we fail to do this, then the words we utter in the liturgy are a lie, and lead only to our condemnation. "You will know them by their fruits,"[25] Jesus tells his followers.

Conclusion—Christ's Ultimate Victory

Ultimately, the Church's ministry to the sick, whether through the sacrament of healing or through the broader ministry that is the responsibility of all the baptized, is nothing less than the bold

[25]Matt 7.16. See also Matt 7.20.

proclamation that the problem of sin and sickness has been solved. It is not that sin and sickness have been eliminated—they obviously continue to exist in this world. What has changed, however, is that, through Christ, they have lost their power. This is what we proclaim in the paschal troparion, which we sing so many times during the season of Pascha:

Christ is risen from the dead, trampling down death by death, and upon those in the tombs bestowing life.

The paschal event changes our entire perspective on the world, on our life, and on healing. Yes, we still all get sick and die, for Christ has not eliminated biological death. Yet now, because of what Christ has accomplished, sickness and death no longer rule, are rendered powerless, because they are no longer the end of life, but a passage to ever fuller life in Christ. Thus the Christian has nothing to fear, because, through the cross, defeat is turned into victory. This is the ultimate meaning of the gospel, the "good news." The Church's healing ministry, including the sacrament of anointing, is but an expression, an affirmation, of this joyful reality!

Who better to teach us this truth than the true Christian who, just like the martyrs of old, passes joyfully through this time of trial in the certainty of the victory that has been assured? This witness is of inestimable value for the Church, for it confirms the truth of the gospel and encourages others to follow. Such was the testimony left to us by Fr Alexander Schmemann, who died after a long struggle with the cancer that eventually took his life. On Thanksgiving Day in 1983, only weeks before his death, he presided over the eucharistic liturgy for the last time and delivered the following sermon:

Everyone capable of thanksgiving is capable of salvation and eternal joy.

Thank you, O Lord, for having accepted this eucharist, which is offered to the Holy Trinity, Father, Son, and Holy Spirit, and which filled our hearts with "the joy, peace and righteousness in the Holy Spirit."

Thank you, O Lord, for having revealed yourself unto us and for giving us the foretaste of your kingdom.

Thank you, O Lord, for having united us to one another, in serving you and your holy Church.

Thank you, O Lord, for having helped us to overcome all difficulties, tensions, passions, and temptations and for having restored peace, mutual love and joy in sharing the communion of the Holy Spirit.

Thank you, O Lord, for the sufferings you bestowed upon us, for they are purifying us from selfishness and remind us of the "one thing needed: your eternal kingdom."

Thank you, O Lord, for this school,[26] where the name of God is proclaimed.

Thank you, O Lord, for our families: husbands, wives and, especially, children, who teach us how to celebrate your holy name, in joy, movement and holy noise.

Thank you, O Lord, for everyone and everything. Great are you, O Lord, and marvelous are your deeds, and no word is sufficient to celebrate your miracles.

Lord, it is good to be here!

Amen.

[26]St Vladimir's Orthodox Theological Seminary, where Fr Alexander served as dean for over twenty years until his death on December 13, 1983.

APPENDIX 1

The Rite of Anointing of the Sick

The Service of Holy Oil, Sung by Seven Priests Assembled in a Church, or in a House

A small table is prepared, and on it is placed a bowl of wheat and a gospel book. An empty vigil lamp is set on the wheat, and seven cotton swabs for anointing are stuck into the wheat surrounding the lamp. Two containers, one with olive oil, the other with water (or red wine), are also placed next to it. Seven presbyters stand around the table, vested in epitrachilia and phelonia and holding candles. The senior priest incenses three times around the table, then the entire church or house, and the people. Then he stands before the table, facing east, and begins, saying:

PRIEST: Blessed is our God, always, now and ever, and unto ages of ages.

READER: Amen. Holy God, Holy Mighty, Holy Immortal, have mercy on us. (3) Glory to the Father, and to the Son, and to the Holy Spirit, now and ever and unto ages of ages. Amen. O most holy Trinity, have mercy on us. Lord, cleanse us from our sins. Master, pardon our transgressions. Holy One, visit and heal our infirmities for your name's sake.

Lord, have mercy. (3)

Our Father, who art in heaven, hallowed be thy name. Thy kingdom come. Thy will be done, on earth as it is in heaven. Give us this day our daily bread; and forgive us our trespasses, as we forgive those who trespass against us; and lead us not into temptation, but deliver us from evil.

PRIEST: For yours is the kingdom, and the power, and the glory, of the Father, and of the Son, and of the Holy Spirit, now and ever, and unto ages of ages.

READER: Amen. Lord, have mercy. (12)

Glory to the Father, and to the Son, and to the Holy Spirit, now and ever, and unto ages of ages. Amen.

Come, let us worship God our King. Come, let us worship and fall down before Christ, our King and our God. Come, let us worship and fall down before the very Christ, our King and our God.

Psalm 143[142]

Hear my prayer, O Lord; give ear to my supplications! In your faithfulness answer me, in your righteousness! Enter not into judgment with your servant; for no man living is righteous before you. For the enemy has pursued me; he has crushed my life to the ground; he has made me sit in darkness like those long dead. Therefore my spirit faints within me; my heart within me is appalled. I remember the days of old, I meditate on all that you have done; I muse on what your hands have wrought. I stretch out my hands to you; my soul thirsts for you like a parched land. Make haste to answer me, O Lord! My spirit fails! Hide not your face from me, lest I be like those who go down to the pit. Let me hear in the morning of your steadfast love, for in you I put my trust. Teach me the way I should go, for to you I lift up my soul. Deliver me, O Lord, from my enemies! I have fled to you for refuge! Teach me to do your will, for you are my God! Let your good Spirit lead me on a level path! For your name's sake, O Lord, preserve my life! In your righteousness bring me out of trouble! And in your steadfast love cut off my enemies, and destroy all my adversaries, for I am your servant.

Glory to the Father, and to the Son, and to the Holy Spirit, now and ever, and unto ages of ages. Amen.

Alleluia, alleluia, alleluia, glory to you, O God. (3)

And the deacon recites the little litany:

DEACON: Again and again, in peace, let us pray to the Lord.

PEOPLE: Lord, have mercy.

DEACON: Help us, save us, have mercy on us, and protect us, O God, by your grace.

PEOPLE: Lord, have mercy.

DEACON: Remembering our most holy, pure, most blessed and glorious Lady, the Theotokos and ever-virgin Mary, with all the saints, let us commit ourselves, and one another, and our whole life, to Christ our God.

PEOPLE: To you, O Lord.

PRIEST: For to you belong all glory, honor, and worship: to the Father and the Son and the Holy Spirit, now and ever, and unto ages of ages.

PEOPLE: Amen.

And the Alleluia is sung in tone 6:

DEACON: Alleluia, alleluia, alleluia.

PEOPLE: Alleluia, alleluia, alleluia.

DEACON, *verse:* O Lord, rebuke me not in your anger, nor chasten me in your wrath. (Ps 6.1)

PEOPLE: Alleluia, alleluia, alleluia.

DEACON, *verse:* Be gracious to me, O Lord, for I am languishing. (Ps 6.2)

PEOPLE: Alleluia, alleluia, alleluia.

Then the troparia are sung:

Have mercy on us, O Lord, have mercy on us. For we sinners, void of all defense, offer to you, as to our Master, this petition: Have mercy on us.

Glory . . .

Have mercy on us, O Lord, for in you have we trusted, and do not be very angry with us, nor remember our iniquities. But look down even now on us, for you are of tender compassion, and deliver us from our enemies. For you are our God, and we are your people. We are all the work of your hand, and we call on your name.

Now and ever . . .

Open to us the door of your loving-kindness, O blessed Theotokos. Because we have set our hope on you, may we not fail, but through you may we be delivered from all adversities: for you are the salvation of all Christians.

Then the reader chants Psalm 51[50]:

Psalm 51[50]

Have mercy on me, O God, according to your steadfast love; according to your abundant mercy blot out my transgressions. Wash me thoroughly from my iniquity, and cleanse me from my sin! For I know my transgressions, and my sin is ever before me. Against you only have I sinned, and done that which is evil in your sight, so that you are justified in your sentence and blameless in your judgment. Behold, I was brought forth in iniquities, and in sins did my mother bear me. Behold, you desire truth in the inward being; therefore teach me wisdom in my secret heart. Purge me with hyssop, and I shall be clean; wash me, and I shall be whiter than snow. Fill me with joy and gladness; let the bones which you have broken rejoice. Hide your face from my sins, and blot out all my iniquities. Create in me a clean heart, O God, and put a new and steadfast spirit within me. Cast me not away from your presence, and take not your Holy Spirit from me. Restore to me the joy of your salvation, and uphold me with a willing spirit. Then I will teach transgressors your ways, and sinners will return to you. Deliver me from blood-guiltiness, O God, the God of my salvation, and my tongue will sing aloud of your deliverance. O Lord, open my lips, and my mouth shall show forth your praise. For you have no delight in sacrifice; were I to give a burnt offering, you would not be pleased. The sacrifice acceptable to God is a broken spirit; a broken and contrite heart, O God, you will not despise. Do good to Zion in your good pleasure; rebuild the walls of Jerusalem; then you will delight in right sacrifices, in burnt offerings and whole burnt offerings; then bulls will be offered on your altar.

Then follows the Canon, in tone 4, whose acrostic is: "The Prayer of the Oil, a Song of Arsenius."

Canon

Ode 1

Hirmos: When of old Israel crossed the Red Sea without getting wet, by the cross-wise stretching forth of Moses' hands, they defeated the forces of Amalek in the wilderness.

Refrain: O merciful Lord, have mercy and heal your suffering servant.

Troparia: With the oil of mercy, O Master, you always make glad both the souls and bodies of men; with oil you preserve the faithful. Even now, with this oil show mercy on those who draw near to you.

Refrain: O merciful Lord, have mercy and heal your suffering servant.

The whole earth, O Lord, is filled with your mercy. Today we shall be anointed with your precious, divine oil; and in faith we ask you: grant us your mercy which passes all understanding.

Glory . . .

Through your apostles, O loving God, you mercifully commanded us to perform your sacred anointing upon your ailing servants. Through their prayers and through the seal of your anointing, have mercy on us all.

Now and ever . . .

Theotokion: O only Pure One, who gave birth to the boundless source of peace, by your ceaseless prayers deliver your servant from infirmities and afflictions, that he(she) may always glorify you.

Ode 3

Hirmos: In you, O Christ, the Church rejoices and cries out: "You are my fortress, O Lord, my refuge and my confirmation!"

Refrain: O merciful Lord, have mercy and heal your suffering servant.

Troparia: You alone are full of wonders! You alone are merciful to the faithful! Grant your grace from above to your ailing servant (name).

Refrain: O merciful Lord, have mercy and heal your suffering servant.

By your divine command, O Lord, of old you showed forth an olive-branch to hold back the flood; now save your suffering servant.

Glory . . .

With the lamp of your divine light, O Christ, in your mercy enlighten through anointing him(her) who in faith hastens to your mercy.

Now and ever . . .

Theotokion: Graciously look down from on high, O Mother of the Creator of all, and through your prayers deliver your suffering servant from sharp afflictions.

Kathisma Hymn (Tone 8)

You are like a divine river of mercy, an inexhaustible source of compassionate mercy, O Bountiful One. Show forth the streams of your divine mercy and heal us all; pour out abundant floods of wonders and wash us all clean: for we always have recourse to you and fervently seek your grace.

and another (Tone 4)

O Physician and Helper of the suffering, O Redeemer and Savior of the sick, O Master and Lord of all, grant healing to your ailing servant. Show compassion, have mercy on him(her) who has grievously sinned, and deliver him(her) from his(her) sins, that he(she) may glorify your divine power.

Ode 4

Hirmos: Seeing you, the Sun of Righteousness, hanging on the cross, the Church stands before you and rightly cries out: "Glory to your power, O Lord."

Refrain: O merciful Lord, have mercy and heal your suffering servant.

Troparia: Like pure chrism, O Savior, you pour out your grace and purify the world: show your divine mercy and compassion upon the bodily wounds of the one who in faith is to be anointed.

Refrain: O merciful Lord, have mercy and heal your suffering servant.

Because you seal the senses of your servant with the joy of the seal of your mercy, O Master, make him(her) impervious to all adverse powers.

Glory . . .

You commanded the sick to summon the godly ministers, to obtain salvation through their prayers and anointing with your oil: O loving God, by your mercy save your suffering servant.

Now and ever . . .

Theotokion: O all-holy, ever-virgin Theotokos, steadfast Protectress and Refuge, Haven and Wall, Ladder and Bulwark: have mercy and compassion upon this suffering servant, for to you alone has he(she) fled for refuge.

Ode 5

Hirmos: You, O my Lord, are the light that has come into the world, the light that turns from the darkness of ignorance those who with faith sing your praise.

Refrain: O merciful Lord, have mercy and heal your suffering servant.

Troparia: You are the endless source of mercy, O Good One: by your divine mercy, O Merciful One, show your mercy upon this suffering servant, for you are compassionate.

Refrain: O merciful Lord, have mercy and heal your suffering servant.

Ineffably you sealed our souls and bodies with your divine image, O Christ: heal us all by your hand.

Glory . . .

In your indescribable love, O supremely good Lord, you accepted anointment with myrrh from the sinful woman: have compassion on your servant.

Now and ever . . .

Theotokion: O all-praised, pure, supremely good Lady, have mercy on those who are about to be anointed with oil, and save your servant.

Ode 6

Hirmos: Cleansed of the blood of demons by the blood which flowed mercifully from your side, the Church cries out to you: "A sacrifice of praise will I offer you, O Lord!"

Refrain: O merciful Lord, have mercy and heal your suffering servant.

Troparia: By your words, O Loving God, you declared anointing for kings and accomplished it through priests: by your seal save also your suffering servant, for you are compassionate.

Refrain: O merciful Lord, have mercy and heal your suffering servant.

Let no bitter demons touch the senses of him(her) who is sealed with your divine anointing, O Savior, but surround him(her) with the shelter of your glory.

Glory . . .

Stretch forth your hand from on high, O God who loves mankind; and having blessed your oil, O Savior, bestow it on your servant for healing and for a release from all ills.

Now and ever . . .

Theotokion: You showed yourself to be a fruitful olive tree in the house of God, O Mother of the Creator, and through you we see the world full of mercy: by your prayers, relieve also the pangs of your suffering servant.

Kontakion (tone 2)

O Fountain of mercy, greatly good One, deliver from every adversity these servants who adore your ineffable mercy, O compassionate One. Deliver them from all affliction, remove their diseases, and grant them divine grace from on high.

Ode 7

Hirmos: Consumed by a burning love of godliness greater than the flame, the children of Abraham in the Persian furnace cried out: "Blessed are you in the temple of your glory, O Lord!"

Refrain: O merciful Lord, have mercy and heal your suffering servant.

Troparia: In your mercy and compassion, O only God and Savior, you heal both the passions of the soul and the failings of the body: restore also this suffering servant and heal him(her).

Refrain: O merciful Lord, have mercy and heal your suffering servant.

When the heads of all are anointed with oil, grant the joy of gladness to this servant, who seeks the mercy of your redemption, O Christ, and bestow the riches of your grace, O Lord.

Glory . . .

Your seal is a sword against demons, O Savior, a fire consuming the passions of the soul through the prayers of the priest. So we, who have received healing, in faith sing praises to you.

Now and ever . . .

Theotokion: O Mother of God, in your womb you worthily contained him who holds all things in the hollow of his hand, and ineffably you gave him birth: we pray you, alleviate the suffering of this servant.

Ode 8

Hirmos: Daniel stretched out his hands and closed the jaws of the lion in the den, and the godly young men quenched the raging fire by girding themselves with virtue and crying out: "Bless the Lord, all you works of the Lord!"

Refrain: O merciful Lord, have mercy and heal your suffering servant.

Troparia: You have mercy on all, O Savior, according to your great and divine mercy. For this reason we all gather together, mystically imitating your desire for compassion and in faith bringing anointing with oil to your servant: you yourself grant him healing.

Refrain: O merciful Lord, have mercy and heal your suffering servant.

By the streams of your mercy, O Christ, and through anointing by your priests, O merciful Lord, wash away his(her) pain and hurt, and the sudden attacks of suffering caused by the violence of passions, so that he(she) may praise you with thanks, O Savior.

Let us bless the Father, the Son, and the Holy Spirit, the Lord.

Your divine mercy has been decreed from on high, O Master, as a sign of condescension and joy: do not take away your mercy, nor despise him(her) who with faith continuously cries: "Bless the Lord, all you works of the Lord!"

Now and ever . . .

Theotokion: Nature accepted your divine birthgiving, O pure one, as a glorious crown, which crushed the hosts of the enemy and defeated its dominion. Crowned, therefore, with the joyful radiance of your grace, O all-praised Lady, we sing praises to you.

Ode 9

Hirmos: From you, an unhewn mountain, O Virgin, was cut Christ, the cornerstone not cut by human hand, who united the natures that had been divided. In joy, therefore, we magnify you, O Theotokos.

Refrain: O merciful Lord, have mercy and heal your suffering servant.

Troparia: Look down from heaven, O compassionate One, and show forth your mercy upon us all. Give now your help and your strength, O God who loves mankind, to him(her) who draws near to you through divine anointing at the hands of your priests.

Refrain: O merciful Lord, have mercy and heal your suffering servant.

Rejoicing, we have seen your divine oil, which you have accepted in your divine condescension, O all-good Savior, and which you distribute as communion to those who have partaken of the divine bath.

Glory . . .

Show compassion, have mercy, O Savior, deliver from terror and pain, rescue from the arrows of the Evil One the souls and bodies of your servants: for you are a merciful Lord, who heals by your divine grace.

Now and ever . . .

Theotokion: As you receive the hymns and prayers of your servants, O Virgin, so also deliver from grievous suffering and pain him(her) who, through us, flees to your divine protection, O all-pure one.

It is truly fitting to bless you, O Theotokos, ever blessed and most pure and the Mother of our God. More honorable than the Cherubim and beyond compare more glorious than the Seraphim, without corruption you gave birth to God the Word: true Theotokos, we magnify you.

Exaposteilarion

As we gather in your holy temple to anoint your suffering servant(s) with divine oil, O good One, look with divine mercy upon our petitions.

Praises (tone 4)

Let everything that breathes praise the Lord! Praise the Lord from the heavens! Praise him in the highest! To you, O God, is due a song!

Praise him, all his angels! Praise him, all his hosts! To you, O God, is due a song!

Stichera: By this holy oil, O God who loves and forgives mankind, through your apostles you have given your grace to heal the wounds and infirmities of all. Have mercy now upon him(her) who with faith approaches your oil; in your compassion, O Lord, sanctify him(her), have mercy on him(her), cleanse him(her) from every disease, and grant him(her) your incorruptible food.

Verse: Praise him with timbrel and dance! Praise him with strings and pipe!

You are compassionate, O ineffable One; by your invisible hand, O God who loves mankind, you have sealed our senses with your divine oil. Look down from heaven upon him(her) who appeals to you in faith and asks for the forgiveness of his(her) sins. Grant healing of both soul and body, so that he(she) may glorify you and magnify your power.

Verse: Praise him with sounding cymbals! Praise him with loud clashing cymbals! Let everything that breathes praise the Lord!

By anointing with your holy oil and through the touch of priests, O God who loves mankind, from on high sanctify your servant. Free him(her) from his(her) infirmities; purge his(her) spirit. Wash him(her), O Savior, and deliver him(her) from every cunning temptation. Assuage his(her) suffering; avert all obstacles; remove all afflictions, for you are compassionate and merciful.

Glory to the Father, and to the Son, and to the Holy Spirit, now and ever, and unto ages of ages. Amen.

Theotokion: O most pure palace of the King, O greatly honored one, I pray you to cleanse my mind polluted by every sin, and to make it into an acceptable dwelling for the most-divine Trinity: so that I, your unprofitable servant, may be saved and praise your power and your infinite mercy.

READER: Holy God, Holy Mighty, Holy Immortal, have mercy on us. (3)

Glory to the Father, and to the Son, and to the Holy Spirit, now and ever and unto ages of ages. Amen.

O most holy Trinity, have mercy on us. Lord, cleanse us from our sins. Master, pardon our transgressions. Holy One, visit and heal our infirmities for your name's sake.

Lord, have mercy. (3)

Our Father, who art in heaven, hallowed be thy name. Thy kingdom come. Thy will be done, on earth as it is in heaven. Give us this day our daily bread; and forgive us our trespasses, as we forgive those who trespass against us; and lead us not into temptation, but deliver us from evil.

PRIEST: For yours is the kingdom, and the power, and the glory, of the Father, and of the Son, and of the Holy Spirit, now and ever, and unto ages of ages.

Troparion (tone 4)

You alone are a speedy helper, O Christ: speedily visit from on high your suffering servant. Deliver him(her) from diseases and acute suffering; raise him(her) up to sing praises to you and ceaselessly to glorify you, the God who alone loves mankind, through the prayers of the Theotokos.

Then the deacon, or the principal priest, recites the following litany:

Litany

DEACON: In peace, let us pray to the Lord.

PEOPLE: Lord, have mercy.

DEACON: For the peace from above, and for the salvation of our souls, let us pray to the Lord.

PEOPLE: Lord, have mercy.

DEACON: For this holy house, and for those who enter it with faith, reverence, and the fear of God, let us pray to the Lord.

PEOPLE: Lord, have mercy.

DEACON: That he will bless this oil through the power, operation, and descent of the Holy Spirit, let us pray to the Lord.

PEOPLE: Lord, have mercy.

DEACON: For the servant of God (name), that God may visit him(her), and that the grace of the Holy Spirit may come upon him(her), let us pray to the Lord.

PEOPLE: Lord, have mercy.

DEACON: That he will deliver him(her) and us from all affliction, wrath, danger, and distress, let us pray to the Lord.

PEOPLE: Lord, have mercy.

DEACON: Help us, save us, have mercy on us, and protect us, O God, by your grace.

PEOPLE: Lord, have mercy.

DEACON: Remembering our most holy, pure, most blessed and glorious Lady, the Theotokos and ever-virgin Mary, with all the saints, let us commit ourselves, and one another, and our whole life to Christ our God.

PEOPLE: To you, O Lord.

Then the principal priest recites the "Prayer of the Oil" over the vigil lamp, into which he pours some oil. In some churches, some wine is also mixed into the oil. The other priests recite the same prayer silently.

Prayer of the Oil

O Lord, in your mercy and compassion, you heal the afflictions of our souls and bodies: sanctify now this oil, O Master, that it may bring healing to those who are anointed with it, relief from every passion, from every sickness of flesh and spirit, and from all evil; and so that your holy name may be glorified, of the Father, and of the Son, and of the Holy Spirit, now and ever, and unto ages of ages.

PEOPLE: Amen.

The following troparia are sung:

Troparia

Tone 4

You alone are a speedy helper, O Christ: swiftly visit from on high your suffering servant. Deliver him(her) from disease and bitter pain; raise him(her) up to sing praises to you and ceaselessly to glorify you, the only loving God, through the prayers of the Theotokos.

Spiritually blind, O Christ, I come to you as did the man born blind, and in repentance I call out to you: "Make your light to shine upon those in darkness!"

Tone 3

My soul is paralyzed by many sins and evil deeds; yet by your divine intercession, O Lord, raise up my soul, as of old you raised the paralytic, so that being saved I may cry to you: "Grant me healing, O compassionate Christ!"

St James, tone 2

As a disciple of the Lord, O righteous James, you received the gospel; as a martyr, you have the ultimate victory; as a brother of the Lord, you have boldness; as a hierarch, you have the power of prayer: Implore Christ our God that he may save our souls.

St James, tone 4

The only-begotten Word of God the Father, who in these days has dwelt among us, appointed you, O divine James, to be the first shepherd and teacher of the church in Jerusalem, and a faithful steward of spiritual mysteries: therefore, O apostle, we all honor you.

St Nicholas, tone 3

To the people of Myra, O holy one, you showed yourself as priest: fulfilling the gospel of Christ, O holy one, you laid down your life for your people and saved the innocent from death. Therefore you are canonized as a great initiate in the grace of God.

St Demetrios, tone 3

The world has found in you a champion great in suffering, O victorious one, who put the pagans to flight. For as you humbled the pride of Lyaios and encouraged Nestor to strive for the prize, O Saint Demetrios, pray to Christ our God that he will grant us great mercy.

St Panteleimon, tone 3

O holy victor and healer Panteleimon, pray to the merciful God that he will grant our souls forgiveness of sins.

Unmercenary Saints, tone 8

O holy unmercenaries and wonderworkers, visit our infirmities. Freely you have received, freely give to us.

St John the Theologian, tone 2

Who shall declare your greatness, O virgin one? For you are rich in wonders and pour forth streams of healing. You intercede for our souls, for you are a theologian and friend of Christ.

Theotokion, tone 2

O fervent intercession and impregnable wall, O fountain of mercy and refuge of the world, fervently we call out to you: Come to our aid, O Lady; deliver us from adversity, O Theotokos, who alone are a speedy defender.

First Anointing

Prokeimenon

DEACON: Let us be attentive.

FIRST PRIEST: Peace be to all.

READER: And to your spirit.

DEACON: Wisdom.

READER: The Prokeimenon in the first tone. Let your steadfast love, O Lord, be upon us, even as we hope on you. (Ps 33[32].22)

verse: Rejoice in the Lord, O you righteous! Praise befits the upright. (Ps 33[32].1)

Epistle (James 5.10–16)

DEACON: Wisdom.

READER: The reading is from the General Epistle of St James.

DEACON: Let us be attentive.

READER: Brethren, as an example of suffering and patience, take the prophets who spoke in the name of the Lord. Behold, we call those happy who were steadfast. You have heard of the steadfastness of Job, and you have seen the purpose of the Lord, how the Lord is compassionate and merciful.

But above all, my brethren, do not swear, either by heaven or by earth or with any other oath, but let your yes be yes and your no be no, that you may not fall under condemnation.

Is any one among you suffering? Let him pray. Is any cheerful? Let him sing praise. Is any among you sick? Let him call for the elders of the church, and let them pray over him, anointing him with oil in the name of the Lord; and the prayer of faith will save the sick man, and the Lord will raise him up; and if he has committed sins, he will be forgiven. Therefore confess your sins to one another, and pray for one another, that you may be healed. The prayer of a righteous man has great power in its effects.

PRIEST: Peace be to you.

READER: And to your spirit. Alleluia, alleluia, alleluia. *(tone 8)*

PEOPLE: Alleluia, alleluia, alleluia.

READER, *verse:* I will sing of loyalty and of justice; to you, O Lord, I will sing. (Ps 101[100].1)

PEOPLE: Alleluia, alleluia, alleluia.

Gospel (Luke 10.25–37)

DEACON: Wisdom. Attend. Let us listen to the Holy Gospel.

PRIEST: Peace be to all.

PEOPLE: And to your spirit.

PRIEST: The reading is from the Holy Gospel according to Saint Luke.

PEOPLE: Glory to you, O Lord, glory to you.

DEACON: Let us be attentive.

FIRST PRIEST: At that time, a lawyer stood up to put him to the test, saying: "Teacher, what shall I do to inherit eternal life?" He said to him, "What is written in the law? How do you read?" and he answered, "You shall love the Lord your God with all your heart, and with all your soul, and with all your strength, and with all your mind; and your neighbor as yourself." And he said to him, "You have answered right; do this, and you will live."

But he, desiring to justify himself, said to Jesus, "And who is my neighbor?" Jesus replied, "A man was going down from Jerusalem to Jericho, and he fell among robbers, who stripped and beat him, and departed, leaving him half dead. Now by chance a priest was going down that road; and when he saw him he passed by on the other side. So likewise a Levite, when he came to the place and saw him, passed by on the other side. But a Samaritan, as he journeyed, came to where he was; and when he saw him, he had compassion, and went to him and bound up his wounds, pouring on oil and wine; then he set him on his own beast and brought him to an inn, and took care of him. And the next day he took out two denarii and gave them to the innkeeper, saying, 'Take care of him; and whatever more you spend, I will repay you when I come back.' Which of these, do you think, proved neighbor to the man who fell among robbers?" He said, "The one who showed mercy on him." And Jesus said to him, "Go and do likewise."

PEOPLE: Glory to you, O Lord, glory to you.

Then the deacon recites the litany:

Litany

DEACON: Have mercy on us, O God, in your great loving-kindness: we pray you, hear us, and have mercy.

PEOPLE: Lord, have mercy. (3)

DEACON: Again we pray for mercy, life, peace, health, salvation, and remission of sins of the servant of God (name).

PEOPLE: Lord, have mercy. (3)

DEACON: That he(she) may be pardoned every transgression, let us pray to the Lord.

PEOPLE: Lord, have mercy. (3)

PRIEST: For you are a merciful God who loves mankind, and to you we give glory, to the Father, and to the Son, and to the Holy Spirit, now and ever, and unto ages of ages.

PEOPLE: Amen.

Prayer

DEACON: Let us pray to the Lord.

PEOPLE: Lord, have mercy.

FIRST PRIEST: You are without beginning, eternal, holy of holies, who sent down your only-begotten Son to heal every disease and every infirmity of our souls and bodies: send down your Holy Spirit and sanctify this oil; and grant that it may bring full pardon from sin to your servant (name) who is to be anointed, and the inheritance of the kingdom of Heaven.

Some say the prayer only to here, adding the exclamation "For you are merciful and save us . . . " Others recite the prayer to the end.

For you are a great and wonderful God: you keep your covenant and your mercy toward those who love you, granting forgiveness of sins through your holy Child, Jesus Christ, who grants us a new birth from sin, who gives light to the blind, who raises up those who are cast down, who loves the righteous and shows mercy to sinners, who leads us out of darkness and the shadow of death, saying to those in chains, "Go forth," and to those who sit in darkness, "Open your eyes." You made the light of the knowledge of his countenance to shine in our hearts when for our sakes he revealed himself upon earth, and dwelt among us. To those who accepted him, he gave the power to become children of God, granting us adoption through the washing of regeneration and removing us from the tyranny of the devil. For it did not please you that we should be cleansed by blood, but by holy oil, so you gave us the image of his Cross, that we might become the flock of Christ, a royal priesthood, a holy nation; and you purified us with water and sanctified us with the Holy Spirit.

Yourself, O Master and Lord, grant us grace in this your ministry, as you gave it to Moses, your servant, to Samuel, your beloved, to John, your chosen one, and to all those who, from generation to generation, have been well-pleasing to you. So also make us to be ministers of the new covenant of your Son over this oil, which you have acquired through the precious blood of your Christ; so that putting aside our worldly desires, we may die to sin and live in righteousness, clothed in him through the anointing with the oil of sanctification which we are about to undergo.

Let this oil, O Lord, become the oil of gladness, the oil of sanctification, a royal robe, an armor of might, the averting of every
work of the devil, an unassailable seal, the joy of the heart, and
eternal rejoicing. Grant that those who are anointed with this oil
of regeneration may be fearsome to their adversaries, and that
they may shine with the radiance of your saints, having neither
stain nor defect, and that they may attain your everlasting rest
and receive the prize of their high calling. For you are merciful
and save us, O God, our God, and to you we give glory, together
with your only-begotten Son and your all-holy, good, and life-giving Spirit: now and ever, and unto ages of ages.

PEOPLE: Amen.

*After the prayer, the priest takes one of the cotton swabs, dips it
into the holy oil, and anoints the sick person, crosswise, on the
brows, the nostrils, the cheeks, the lips, the breast, and on both
sides of the hands. As he anoints the sick person, he recites the following prayer:*

Prayer of Anointing

O holy Father, Physician of souls and bodies, who sent your only-
begotten Son, our Lord Jesus Christ, who heals every infirmity
and delivers from death: heal also your servant (name) from the
infirmities of body and soul which afflict him(her), and enliven
him(her) with the grace of your Christ; through the prayers of our
most-holy Lady, the Theotokos and ever-virgin Mary; through
the intercessions of the honorable, bodiless powers of heaven;
through the power of the precious and life-giving cross; through
the protection of the honorable, glorious prophet, forerunner,
and baptist, John; of the holy, glorious, and most-blessed apos-

added
in later
practice

tles; of the holy, glorious, victorious martyrs; of our venerable and God-bearing fathers; of the holy unmercenary physicians, Cosmas and Damian, Cyrus and John, Panteleimon and Hermolaus, Sampson and Diomedes, Photius and Anicetas; of the holy and righteous ancestors of God, Joachim and Anna; and of all the saints.) For you are the fountain of healing, O our God, and to you we give glory, to the Father, and the Son, and the Holy Spirit, now and ever, and unto ages of ages. Amen.

This prayer is recited by each of the priests after he has read the gospel and the prayer, as he anoints the sick person with oil.

Second Anointing

Prokeimenon

DEACON: Let us be attentive.

SECOND PRIEST: Peace be to all.

READER: And to your spirit.

DEACON: Wisdom.

READER: The Prokeimenon in the second tone. The Lord is my strength and my song; he has become my salvation. (Ps 118[117].14)

verse: The Lord has chastened me sorely, but he has not given me over to death. (Ps 118[117].18)

Epistle (Rom 15.1–7)

DEACON: Wisdom!

READER: The reading is from the Epistle of the holy Apostle Paul to the Romans.

DEACON: Let us be attentive.

READER: Brethren, we who are strong ought to bear with the failings of the weak, and not to please ourselves; let each of us please his neighbor for his good, to edify him. For Christ did not please himself; but, as it is written, "The reproaches of those who reproached you fell on me." For whatever was written in former days was written for our instruction, that by steadfastness and by the encouragement of the scriptures we might have hope. May the God of steadfastness and encouragement grant you to live in such harmony with one another, in accord with Christ Jesus, that together you may with one voice glorify the God and Father of our Lord Jesus Christ.

Welcome one another, therefore, as Christ has welcomed you, for the glory of God.

PRIEST: Peace be to you.

READER: And to your spirit. Alleluia, alleluia, alleluia. *(tone 5)*

PEOPLE: Alleluia, alleluia, alleluia.

READER, *verse:* I will sing of your steadfast love, O Lord, for ever. (Ps 89[88].1)

PEOPLE: Alleluia, alleluia, alleluia.

Gospel (Luke 19.1–10)

DEACON: Wisdom. Attend. Let us listen to the Holy Gospel.

PRIEST: Peace be to all.

PEOPLE: And to your spirit.

PRIEST: The reading is from the Holy Gospel according to Saint Luke.

PEOPLE: Glory to you, O Lord, glory to you.

DEACON: Let us be attentive.

SECOND PRIEST: At that time, he entered Jericho and was passing through. And there was a man named Zacchaeus; he was a chief tax collector, and rich. And he sought to see who Jesus was, but could not, on account of the crowd, because he was small of stature. So he ran on ahead and climbed up into a sycamore tree to see him, for he was to pass that way. And when Jesus came to the place, he looked up and said to him, "Zacchaeus, make haste and come down; for I must stay at your house today." So he made haste and came down, and received him joyfully. And when they saw it they all murmured, "He has gone in to be the guest of a man who is a sinner." And Zacchaeus stood and said to the Lord, "Behold, Lord, the half of my goods I give to the poor; and if I have defrauded anyone of anything, I restore it fourfold." And Jesus said to him, "Today salvation has come to this house, since he also is a son of Abraham. For the Son of Man came to seek and to save the lost."

PEOPLE: Glory to you, O Lord, glory to you.

Then the deacon recites the litany:

Litany

DEACON: Have mercy on us, O God, in your great loving-kindness: we pray you, hear us, and have mercy.

PEOPLE: Lord, have mercy. (3)

DEACON: Again we pray for mercy, life, peace, health, salvation, and remission of sins of the servant of God (name).

PEOPLE: Lord, have mercy. (3)

DEACON: That he(she) may be pardoned every transgression, let us pray to the Lord.

PEOPLE: Lord, have mercy. (3)

PRIEST: For you are a merciful God who loves mankind, and to you we give glory, to the Father, and to the Son, and to the Holy Spirit, now and ever, and unto ages of ages.

PEOPLE: Amen.

Prayer

DEACON: Let us pray to the Lord.

PEOPLE: Lord, have mercy.

SECOND PRIEST: O great and most-high God, who are worshipped by all creatures, Fountain of wisdom, bottomless Source of goodness, boundless Sea of compassion, Master who loves mankind, God of eternity and of wonders, whom no human mind can comprehend: look down upon us and hear us, your unworthy servants, and send down the gift of your healing and forgiveness of sins wherever, in your great name, we bring this oil; and heal him(her) in the abundance of your mercy. Yea, O Lord, you are easy to be entreated; you alone are merciful and loving; you repent of our evil deeds; you know that our minds are directed toward evil even from our youth; you desire not the death of a sinner, but rather that he should turn from his wickedness and live; for the salvation of sinners you became incarnate; yet, becoming a creature for the sake of your creatures, you remained God. You have said, "I came not to call the righteous but sinners to repentance." You sought the lost sheep. Diligently you searched for the lost coin, and having found it, you said: "Him who comes to me, I will not cast out." You did not despise the sinful woman who washed your precious feet with her tears, for you said, "As often as you fall, rise up and be saved." You also said, "There is joy in heaven over one sinner who repents." Look down from the heights of your dwelling, O compassionate Master, and in this hour cover us, your sinful and unworthy servants, with the shadow of the grace of the Holy Spirit. Come and abide in your servant (name), who acknowledges his(her) sins, and who in faith draws near to you. Accept him(her) in your love for mankind, forgive him(her) if he(she) has sinned in word, deed, or thought, cleanse him(her), purify him(her) from every sin. Ever abide with him(her), protect him(her) all the remaining years of his(her) life, so that, ever walking in your commandments, he(she) may not again become an object of scorn for the devil, and so that your most-holy Name may be glorified in him(her). For you are merciful and save us, O God, our God, and to you we give glory, together with your only-begotten Son and your all-holy, good, and life-giving Spirit, now and ever, and unto ages of ages.

PEOPLE: Amen.

Having completed this prayer, the second priest anoints the sick person with oil, reciting the following prayer:

Prayer of Anointing

O holy Father, Physician of souls and bodies, who sent your only-begotten Son, our Lord Jesus Christ, who heals every infirmity and delivers from death: heal also your servant (name) from the infirmities of body and soul which afflict him(her), and enliven him(her) with the grace of your Christ; through the prayers of our most-holy Lady, the Theotokos and ever-virgin Mary; through the intercessions of the honorable, bodiless powers of heaven; through the power of the precious and life-giving Cross; through the protection of the honorable, glorious prophet, forerunner, and baptist, John; of the holy, glorious, and most-blessed apostles; of the holy, glorious, victorious martyrs; of our venerable and God-bearing fathers; of the holy unmercenary physicians, Cosmas and Damian, Cyrus and John, Panteleimon and Hermolaus, Sampson and Diomedes, Photius and Anicetas; of the holy and righteous ancestors of God, Joachim and Anna; and of all the saints. For you are the fountain of healing, O our God, and to you we give glory, to the Father, and the Son, and the Holy Spirit, now and ever, and unto ages of ages. Amen.

Third Anointing

Prokeimenon

DEACON: Let us be attentive.

THIRD PRIEST: Peace be to all.

READER: And to your spirit.

DEACON: Wisdom.

READER: The prokeimenon in the fourth tone. The Lord is my light and my salvation; whom shall I fear? (Ps 27[26].1)

verse: The Lord is the stronghold of my life; of whom shall I be afraid? *(ibid.)*

Epistle (1 Cor 12.27–13.8)

DEACON: Wisdom!

READER: The reading is from the First Epistle of the holy Apostle Paul to the Corinthians.

DEACON: Let us be attentive.

READER: Brethren, you are the body of Christ and individually members of it. And God has appointed in the church first apostles, second prophets, third teachers, then workers of miracles, then healers, helpers, administrators, speakers in various kinds of tongues. Are all apostles? Are all prophets? Are all teachers? Do all work miracles? Do all possess gifts of healing? Do all speak with tongues? Do all interpret? But earnestly desire the higher gifts.

And I will show you a still more excellent way.

If I speak in the tongues of men and of angels, but have not love, I am a noisy gong or a clanging cymbal. And if I have prophetic powers, and understand all mysteries and all knowledge, and if I have all faith, so as to move mountains, but have not love, I am nothing. If I give away all I have, and if I deliver my body to be burned, but have not love, I gain nothing.

Love is patient and kind; love is not jealous or boastful; it is not arrogant or rude. Love does not insist on its own way; it is not irritable or resentful; it does not rejoice at wrong, but rejoices in the right. Love bears all things, believes all things, endures all things. Love never ends.

PRIEST: Peace be to you.

READER: And to your spirit. Alleluia, alleluia, alleluia. *(tone 2)*

PEOPLE: Alleluia, alleluia, alleluia.

READER, *verse:* In you, O Lord, do I seek refuge; let me never be put to shame. (Ps 31[30].1)

PEOPLE: Alleluia, alleluia, alleluia.

Gospel (Matt 10.1, 5–8)

DEACON: Wisdom. Attend. Let us listen to the Holy Gospel.

PRIEST: Peace be to all.

PEOPLE: And to your spirit.

PRIEST: The reading is from the Holy Gospel according to Saint Matthew.

PEOPLE: Glory to you, O Lord, glory to you.

DEACON: Let us be attentive.

THIRD PRIEST: At that time, he called to him his twelve disciples and gave them authority over unclean spirits, to cast them out, and to heal every disease and every infirmity. These twelve Jesus sent out, charging them, "Go nowhere among the Gentiles, and enter no town of the Samaritans, but go rather to the lost sheep of the house of Israel. And preach as you go, saying, 'The kingdom of heaven is at hand.' Heal the sick, raise the dead, cleanse lepers, cast out demons. You received without pay, give without pay."

PEOPLE: Glory to you, O Lord, glory to you.

Then the deacon recites the litany:

Litany

DEACON: Have mercy on us, O God, in your great loving-kindness: we pray you, hear us, and have mercy.

PEOPLE: Lord, have mercy. (3)

DEACON: Again we pray for mercy, life, peace, health, salvation, and remission of sins of the servant of God (name).

PEOPLE: Lord, have mercy. (3)

DEACON: That he(she) may be pardoned every transgression, let us pray to the Lord.

PEOPLE: Lord, have mercy. (3)

PRIEST: For you are a merciful God who loves mankind, and to you we give glory, to the Father, and to the Son, and to the Holy Spirit, now and ever, and unto ages of ages.

PEOPLE: Amen.

Prayer

DEACON: Let us pray to the Lord.

PEOPLE: Lord, have mercy.

THIRD PRIEST: O Master almighty, holy King, you chastise but do not kill; you raise the fallen and restore those who are cast down; you relieve our bodily afflictions: we beg you, O our God, to direct your mercy upon this oil, and upon all who shall be anointed with it in your Name, that it may be for the healing of their souls and bodies, for purification, and for the removal of every passion, every disease and infirmity, and every defilement of body and spirit. Yea, Lord, send down from heaven your healing power: touch the bodies; quench the fever; ease the suffering; and drive away every hidden ailment. Be the physician of your servant (name): raise him(her) up from his(her) bed of sickness, from the bed of affliction, whole and fully cured, granting him(her), through your Church, that which is well-pleasing to you and accomplishes your will. For you are merciful and save us, O God, our God, and to you we give glory, together with your only-begotten Son and your all-holy, good, and life-giving Spirit, now and ever, and unto ages of ages.

PEOPLE: Amen.

Having completed this prayer, the third priest anoints the sick person with oil, reciting the following prayer:

Prayer of Anointing

O holy Father, Physician of souls and bodies, who sent your only-begotten Son, our Lord Jesus Christ, who heals every infirmity and delivers from death: heal also your servant (name) from the infirmities of body and soul which afflict him(her), and enliven him(her) with the grace of your Christ; through the prayers of our most-holy Lady, the Theotokos and ever-virgin Mary; through the intercessions of the honorable, bodiless powers of heaven;

through the power of the precious and life-giving cross; through the protection of the honorable, glorious prophet, forerunner, and baptist, John; of the holy, glorious, and most-blessed apostles; of the holy, glorious, victorious martyrs; of our venerable and God-bearing fathers; of the holy unmercenary physicians, Cosmas and Damian, Cyrus and John, Panteleimon and Hermolaus, Sampson and Diomedes, Photius and Anicetas; of the holy and righteous ancestors of God, Joachim and Anna; and of all the saints.

For you are the fountain of healing, O our God, and to you we give glory, to the Father, and the Son, and the Holy Spirit, now and ever, and unto ages of ages. Amen.

Fourth Anointing

Prokeimenon

DEACON: Let us be attentive.

FOURTH PRIEST: Peace be to all.

READER: And to your spirit.

DEACON: Wisdom.

READER: The prokeimenon in the fourth tone. Incline your ear to me; answer me speedily in the day when I call! (Ps 102[101].2)

verse: Hear my prayer, O Lord; let my cry come to you! (Ps 102[101].1)

Epistle (2 Cor 6.16–7.1)

DEACON: Wisdom!

READER: The reading is from the Second Epistle of the holy Apostle Paul to the Corinthians.

DEACON: Let us be attentive.

READER: Brethren, you are the temple of the living God; as God said, "I will live in them and move among them, and I will be their God, and they shall be my people. Therefore come out from them, and be separate from them, says the Lord, and touch nothing unclean; then I will welcome you, and I will be a father to you, and you shall be my sons and daughters, says the Lord almighty." Since we have these promises, beloved, let us cleanse ourselves from every defilement of body and spirit, and make holiness perfect in the fear of God.

PRIEST: Peace be to you.

READER: And to your spirit. Alleluia, alleluia, alleluia. *(tone 2)*

PEOPLE: Alleluia, alleluia, alleluia.

READER, *verse:* I waited patiently for the Lord; he inclined his ear to me and heard my cry. (Ps 40[39].1)

PEOPLE: Alleluia, alleluia, alleluia.

Gospel (Matt 8.14–23)

DEACON: Wisdom. Attend. Let us listen to the Holy Gospel.

PRIEST: Peace be to all.

PEOPLE: And to your spirit.

PRIEST: The reading is from the Holy Gospel according to Saint Matthew.

PEOPLE: Glory to you, O Lord, glory to you.

DEACON: Let us be attentive.

FOURTH PRIEST: At that time, when Jesus entered Peter's house, he saw his mother-in-law lying sick with a fever; he touched her hand, and the fever left her, and she arose and served him. That evening they brought to him many who were possessed with demons; and he cast out the spirits with a word, and healed all who were sick. This was to fulfill what was spoken by the prophet Isaiah, "He took our infirmities and bore our diseases." Now when Jesus saw great crowds around him, he gave orders to go over to the other side. And a scribe came up and said to him, "Teacher, I will follow you wherever you go." And Jesus said to him, "Foxes have holes, and birds of the air have nests; but the Son of Man has nowhere to lay his head." Another of his disciples said to him, "Lord, let me first go and bury my father." But Jesus said to him, "Follow me, and leave the dead to bury their own dead." And when he got into the boat, his disciples followed him.

PEOPLE: Glory to you, O Lord, glory to you.

Then the deacon recites the litany:

Litany

DEACON: Have mercy on us, O God, in your great loving-kindness: we pray you, hear us, and have mercy.

PEOPLE: Lord, have mercy. (3)

DEACON: Again we pray for mercy, life, peace, health, salvation, and remission of sins of the servant of God (name).

PEOPLE: Lord, have mercy. (3)

DEACON: That he(she) may be pardoned every transgression, let us pray to the Lord.

PEOPLE: Lord, have mercy. (3)

PRIEST: For you are a merciful God who loves mankind, and to you we give glory, to the Father, and to the Son, and to the Holy Spirit, now and ever, and unto ages of ages.

PEOPLE: Amen.

Prayer

DEACON: Let us pray to the Lord.

PEOPLE: Lord, have mercy.

FOURTH PRIEST: O good Lord who loves mankind, compassionate and greatly merciful, abundant in mercy and rich in goodness, Father of mercies and God of all consolation, who through the apostles has given us power to heal the infirmities of your people through oil and prayer: make this oil to be for the healing of those who are anointed with it, for relief from every disease and all sickness, for deliverance from evil of those who in hope await salvation from you. Yea, O Master, Lord, our God almighty, we entreat you to save us all. O only Physician of our souls and bodies, sanctify us all. You heal every disease: heal also your servant (name): raise him(her) up from the bed of sickness, through the mercies of your kindness; visit him(her) with your mercy and compassion; remove from him(her) every illness and infirmity; so that, having been raised up by your mighty hand, he(she) may serve you with all thanksgiving; and that we too, who now share in your ineffable love for humanity, may hymn and glorify you, for you perform great and wondrous deeds, extraordinary and glorious. For you are merciful and save us, O God, our God, and to you we give glory, together with your only-begotten Son and your all-holy, good, and life-giving Spirit: now and ever, and unto ages of ages.

PEOPLE: Amen.

Having completed this prayer, the fourth priest anoints the sick person with oil, reciting the following prayer:

Prayer of Anointing

O holy Father, Physician of souls and bodies, who sent your only-begotten Son, our Lord Jesus Christ, who heals every infirmity and delivers from death: heal also your servant (name) from the infirmities of body and soul which afflict him(her), and enliven him(her) with the grace of your Christ; through the prayers of our most-holy Lady, the Theotokos and ever-virgin Mary; through the intercessions of the honorable, bodiless powers of heaven; through the power of the precious and life-giving cross; through the protection of the honorable, glorious prophet, forerunner, and baptist, John; of the holy, glorious, and most-blessed apostles; of the holy, glorious, victorious martyrs; of our venerable and God-bearing fathers; of the holy unmercenary physicians, Cosmas and Damian, Cyrus and John, Panteleimon and Hermolaus, Sampson and Diomedes, Photius and Anicetas; of the holy and righteous ancestors of God, Joachim and Anna; and of all the saints. For you are the fountain of healing, O our God, and to you we give glory, to the Father, and the Son, and the Holy Spirit, now and ever, and unto ages of ages. Amen.

Fifth Anointing

Prokeimenon

DEACON: Let us be attentive.

FIFTH PRIEST: Peace be to all.

READER: And to your spirit.

DEACON: Wisdom.

READER: The prokeimenon in the fifth tone. Do you, O Lord, protect us, guard us ever from this generation. (Ps 12[11].7)

verse: Help, Lord; for there is no longer any that is godly. (Ps 12[11].1)

Epistle (2 Cor 1.8–11)

DEACON: Wisdom!

READER: The reading is from the Second Epistle of the holy Apostle Paul to the Corinthians.

DEACON: Let us be attentive.

READER: For we do not want you to be ignorant, brethren, of the affliction we experienced in Asia; for we were so utterly, unbearably crushed that we despaired of life itself. Why, we felt that we had received the sentence of death; but that was to make us rely not on ourselves but on God who raises the dead; he delivered us from so deadly a peril, and he will deliver us; on him we have set our hope that he will deliver us again. You also must help us by prayer, so that many will give thanks on our behalf for the blessing granted us in answer to many prayers.

PRIEST: Peace be to you.

READER: And to your spirit. Alleluia, alleluia, alleluia. *(tone 1)*

PEOPLE: Alleluia, alleluia, alleluia.

READER, *verse:* I will sing of your steadfast love, O Lord, for ever. (Ps 89[88].1)

PEOPLE: Alleluia, alleluia, alleluia.

Gospel (Matt 25.1–13)

DEACON: Wisdom. Attend. Let us listen to the Holy Gospel.

PRIEST: Peace be to all.

PEOPLE: And to your spirit.

PRIEST: The reading is from the Holy Gospel according to Saint Matthew.

PEOPLE: Glory to you, O Lord, glory to you.

DEACON: Let us be attentive.

FIFTH PRIEST: The Lord spoke this parable: "Then the kingdom of heaven shall be compared to ten maidens who took their lamps and went to meet the bridegroom. Five of them were foolish, and five were wise. For when the foolish took their lamps, they took no oil with them; but the wise took flasks of oil with their lamps. As the bridegroom was delayed, they all slumbered and slept. But at midnight there was a cry, 'Behold, the bridegroom! Come out to meet him.' Then all those maidens rose and trimmed their lamps. And the foolish said to the wise, 'Give us some of your oil, for our lamps are going out.' But the wise replied, 'Perhaps there will not be enough for us and for you; go rather to the dealers and buy for yourselves.' And while they went to buy, the bridegroom came, and those who were ready went in with him to the marriage feast; and the door was shut. Afterward the other maidens came also, saying, 'Lord, Lord, open to us.' But he replied, 'Truly, I say to you, I do not know you.' Watch therefore, for you know neither the day nor the hour.'"

PEOPLE: Glory to you, O Lord, glory to you.

Then the deacon recites the litany:

Litany

DEACON: Have mercy on us, O God, in your great loving-kindness: we pray you, hear us, and have mercy.

PEOPLE: Lord, have mercy. (3)

DEACON: Again we pray for mercy, life, peace, health, salvation, and remission of sins of the servant of God (name).

PEOPLE: Lord, have mercy. (3)

DEACON: That he(she) may be pardoned every transgression, let us pray to the Lord.

PEOPLE: Lord, have mercy. (3)

PRIEST: For you are a merciful God who loves mankind, and to you we give glory, to the Father, and to the Son, and to the Holy Spirit, now and ever, and unto ages of ages.

PEOPLE: Amen.

Prayer

DEACON: Let us pray to the Lord.

PEOPLE: Lord, have mercy.

FIFTH PRIEST: O Lord our God, you chastise and heal us again; you raise up the beggar from the earth and exalt the poor from the dunghill. O Father of orphans, Refuge of the storm-tossed, and Physician of the sick, easily you bore our diseases and took on our infirmities. Joyfully you show mercy, passing over our transgressions and taking away our unrighteousness; you are quick to help and slow to anger. You breathed on your disciples and said, "Receive the Holy Spirit: if you forgive the sins of any, they are forgiven." You accept the repentance of sinners and have authority to forgive many and grievous sins; you grant healing to all who experience weakness and prolonged illness. You have also called me, your humble, sinful, and unworthy servant, entangled in many sins and wallowing in passions, to the holy and great degree of priesthood, and to enter beyond the inner veil into the holy of holies, which the holy angels desire to approach, and to hear the voice of the Lord God, to behold the manifestation of the holy offering with my own eyes, and to take joy in the divine and sacred liturgy. Grant me the ability, as a priest, to administer your heavenly mysteries, and to offer you gifts and sacrifices for our sins, and for the ignorance of your people, and act as mediator for your reason-endowed sheep, so that you, in your great and ineffable love for humanity, may blot out their transgressions. On this holy day and at this hour, and at every time and place, O exceedingly good King, incline your ear to my prayer and receive the voice of my supplication: grant healing to your servant (name), who lies in sickness of both soul and body; grant him(her) forgiveness of his(her) sins and pardon of his(her) transgressions, both voluntary and involuntary. Heal his(her) incurable wounds, and every disease, and all infirmity. Grant healing to his(her) soul, as you touched Peter's mother-in-law, and the fever left her, and she arose and served you. Grant also healing to your servant (name), and release from all deadly suffering, O Master, remembering your abundant compassion and mercy. Remember that the human mind always inclines toward evil, even from youth, and that no one sinless is to be found upon the earth; for you alone are sinless, who came down and saved the human race and freed us from bondage to the enemy. For if you enter into judgment with your servant, no one shall be found without stain, but every mouth shall be sealed, unable to offer excuse; for before you our righteousness is like a cast-off rag. Therefore do not remember the offenses of our youth, O Lord, for you are the hope of the hopeless, the repose of those who labor and are weighed down with sin; and to you we give glory, together with your Father, who is without beginning, and your all-holy, good, and life-giving Spirit: now and ever, and unto ages of ages.

PEOPLE: Amen.

Having completed this prayer, the fifth priest anoints the sick person with oil, reciting the following prayer:

Prayer of Anointing

O holy Father, Physician of souls and bodies, who sent your only-begotten Son, our Lord Jesus Christ, who heals every infirmity and delivers from death: heal also your servant (name) from the infirmities of body and soul which afflict him(her), and enliven him(her) with the grace of your Christ; through the prayers of our most-holy Lady, the Theotokos and ever-virgin Mary; through the intercessions of the honorable, bodiless powers of heaven; through the power of the precious and life-giving cross; through the protection of the honorable, glorious prophet, forerunner, and baptist, John; of the holy, glorious, and most-blessed apostles; of the holy, glorious, victorious martyrs; of our venerable and God-bearing fathers; of the holy unmercenary physicians, Cosmas and Damian, Cyrus and John, Panteleimon and Hermolaus, Sampson and Diomedes, Photius and Anicetas; of the holy and righteous ancestors of God, Joachim and Anna; and of all the saints. For you are the fountain of healing, O our God, and to you we give glory, to the Father, and the Son, and the Holy Spirit, now and ever, and unto ages of ages. Amen.

Sixth Anointing

Prokeimenon

DEACON: Let us be attentive.

SIXTH PRIEST: Peace be to all.

READER: And to your spirit.

DEACON: Wisdom.

READER: The prokeimenon in the sixth tone. Have mercy, O Lord, according to your steadfast love. (Ps 51[50].1)

verse: Create in me a clean heart, O God, and put a new and right spirit within me. (Ps 51[50].10)

Epistle (Gal 5.22–6.2)

DEACON: Wisdom!

READER: The reading is from the Epistle of the holy Apostle Paul to the Galatians.

DEACON: Let us be attentive.

READER: Brethren, the fruit of the Spirit is love, joy, peace, patience, kindness, goodness, faithfulness, gentleness, self-control; against such there is no law. And those who belong to Christ have crucified the flesh with its passions and desires. If we live by the Spirit, let us also walk by the Spirit. Let us have no self-conceit, no provoking of one another, no envy of one another.

Brethren, if a man is overtaken in any trespass, you who are spiritual should restore him in a spirit of gentleness. Look to yourself, lest you too be tempted. Bear one another's burdens, and so fulfill the law of Christ.

PRIEST: Peace be to you.

READER: And to your spirit. Alleluia, alleluia, alleluia. *(tone 6)*

PEOPLE: Alleluia, alleluia, alleluia.

READER, *verse:* Blessed is the man who fears the Lord, who greatly delights in his commandments! (Ps 112[111].1)

PEOPLE: Alleluia, alleluia, alleluia.

Gospel (Matt 15.21–28)

DEACON: Wisdom. Attend. Let us listen to the Holy Gospel.

PRIEST: Peace be to all.

PEOPLE: And to your spirit.

PRIEST: The reading is from the Holy Gospel according to Saint Matthew.

PEOPLE: Glory to you, O Lord, glory to you.

DEACON: Let us be attentive.

SIXTH PRIEST: At that time, Jesus went away from there and withdrew to the district of Tyre and Sidon. And behold, a Canaanite woman from that region came out and cried, "Have mercy on me, O Lord, Son of David; my daughter is severely possessed by a demon." But he did not answer her a word. And his disciples came and begged him, saying, "Send her away, for she is crying after us." He answered, "I was sent only to the lost sheep of the house of Israel." But she came and knelt before him, saying, "Lord, help me." And he answered, "It is not fair to take the children's bread and throw it to the dogs." She said, "Yes, Lord, yet even the dogs eat the crumbs that fall from their masters' table." Then Jesus answered her, "O woman, great is your faith! Be it done for you as you desire." And her daughter was healed instantly.

PEOPLE: Glory to you, O Lord, glory to you.

Then the deacon recites the litany:

Litany

DEACON: Have mercy on us, O God, in your great lovingkindness: we pray you, hear us, and have mercy.

PEOPLE: Lord, have mercy. (3)

DEACON: Again we pray for mercy, life, peace, health, salvation, and remission of sins of the servant of God (name).

PEOPLE: Lord, have mercy. (3)

DEACON: That he(she) may be pardoned every transgression, let us pray to the Lord.

PEOPLE: Lord, have mercy. (3)

PRIEST: For you are a merciful God who loves mankind, and to you we give glory, to the Father, and to the Son, and to the Holy Spirit, now and ever, and unto ages of ages.

PEOPLE: Amen.

Prayer

DEACON: Let us pray to the Lord.

PEOPLE: Lord, have mercy.

SIXTH PRIEST: We thank you, O Lord our God, who are good and love mankind, Physician of our souls and bodies, who easily bore our diseases, through whose stripes we have all been healed. O good Shepherd, you came to seek the wandering sheep; you give comfort to the faint-hearted and life to the broken-hearted; you healed the woman who for twelve years had an issue of blood; you freed the daughter of the Canaanite woman from the grievous demon; you forgave the two debtors what they owed and granted forgiveness to the sinful woman; you bestowed healing on the paralytic, as well as the forgiveness of his sins; by a word you justified the publican and accepted the thief at his last confession; you took the sins of the world and nailed them to the cross.

We pray and entreat you, O God: in your goodness, loose, remit, pardon the sins and transgressions of your servant (name), voluntary or involuntary, committed in knowledge or in ignorance, by transgression or through disobedience, whether at night or by day; whether he(she) has been excommunicated by a priest, or cursed by father or mother; whether he(she) has sinned by means of sight, or of smell; through adultery, fornication, or through whatever action of body or spirit he(she) has departed from your will and your holiness. If we also have sinned in this manner, forgive us, for you are a good God, who does not remember evil and who loves humanity: do not allow him(her) or us to fall into an evil way of life, nor to follow an evil path.

Yea, O Lord and Master, at this hour hear the prayer of me, a sinner, on behalf of your servant (name), and overlook all his(her) transgressions, for you are a God who does not remember evil. Deliver him(her) from eternal punishment; fill his(her) mouth with your praise; open his(her) lips that he(she) may glorify your holy Name; stretch forth his(her) hands so that he(she) may fulfill your commandments. Guide his(her) feet aright in the way of your gospel, by your grace strengthening all his(her) members and thoughts. For you are our God, who through your holy apostles gave us a command, saying: "Whatever you bind on earth shall be bound in heaven, and whatever you loose on earth shall be loosed in heaven." And again: "If you forgive the sins of any, they are forgiven; if you retain the sins of any, they are retained." As you heard Ezekiel in the sorrow of his soul, at the hour of his death, and despised not his supplications, so also at this hour give ear to me, your humble, sinful, and unworthy servant. For you are the Lord Jesus Christ who, in your goodness and love for humanity, commanded us to forgive sinners even seventy times seven, and who repents of our wickedness and rejoices over the conversion of those who have gone astray. For as is your majesty, so also is your mercy, and to you we give glory, together with your Father, who is without beginning, and your all-holy, good, and life-giving Spirit: now and ever, and unto ages of ages.

PEOPLE: Amen.

Having completed this prayer, the sixth priest anoints the sick person with oil, reciting the following prayer:

Prayer of Anointing

O holy Father, Physician of souls and bodies, who sent your only-begotten Son, our Lord Jesus Christ, who heals every infirmity and delivers from death: heal also your servant (name) from the infirmities of body and soul which afflict him(her), and enliven him(her) with the grace of your Christ; through the prayers of our most-holy Lady, the Theotokos and ever-virgin Mary; through the intercessions of the honorable, bodiless powers of heaven; through the power of the precious and life-giving cross; through the protection of the honorable, glorious prophet, forerunner, and baptist, John; of the holy, glorious, and most-blessed apostles; of the holy, glorious, victorious martyrs; of our venerable and God-bearing fathers; of the holy unmercenary physicians, Cosmas and Damian, Cyrus and John, Panteleimon and Hermolaus, Sampson and Diomedes, Photius and Anicetas; of the holy and righteous ancestors of God, Joachim and Anna; and of all the saints. For you are the fountain of healing, O our God, and to you we give glory, to the Father, and the Son, and the Holy Spirit, now and ever, and unto ages of ages. Amen.

Seventh Anointing

Prokeimenon

DEACON: Let us be attentive.

SEVENTH PRIEST: Peace be to all.

READER: And to your spirit.

DEACON: Wisdom.

READER: The prokeimenon in the seventh tone. O Lord, rebuke me not in your anger, nor chasten me in your wrath. (Ps 6.1)

verse: Be gracious to me, O Lord, for I am languishing. (Ps 6.2)

Epistle (1 Thess 5.14–23)

DEACON: Wisdom!

READER: The reading is from the First Epistle of the holy Apostle Paul to the Thessalonians.

DEACON: Let us be attentive.

READER: We exhort you, brethren, admonish the idlers, encourage the fainthearted, help the weak, be patient with them all. See that none of you repays evil for evil, but always seek to do good to one another and to all. Rejoice always, pray constantly, give thanks in all circumstances; for this is the will of God in Christ Jesus for you. Do not quench the Spirit, do not despise prophesying, but test everything; hold fast to what is good, abstain from every form of evil.

May the God of peace himself sanctify you wholly; and may your spirit and soul and body be kept sound and blameless at the coming of our Lord Jesus Christ.

PRIEST: Peace be to you.

READER: And to your spirit. Alleluia, alleluia, alleluia. *(tone 7)*

PEOPLE: Alleluia, alleluia, alleluia.

READER, *verse:* The Lord answer you in the day of trouble! The name of the God of Jacob protect you! (Ps 20[19].1)

PEOPLE: Alleluia, alleluia, alleluia.

Gospel (Matt 9.9–13)

DEACON: Wisdom. Attend. Let us listen to the Holy Gospel.

PRIEST: Peace be to all.

PEOPLE: And to your spirit.

PRIEST: The reading is from the Holy Gospel according to Saint Matthew.

PEOPLE: Glory to you, O Lord, glory to you.

DEACON: Let us be attentive.

SEVENTH PRIEST: At that time, as Jesus passed on from there, he saw a man called Matthew sitting at the tax office; and he said to him, "Follow me." And he rose and followed him. And as he sat at table in the house, behold, many tax collectors and sinners came and sat down with Jesus and his disciples. And when the Pharisees saw this, they said to his disciples, "Why does your teacher eat with tax collectors and sinners?" But when he heard it, he said, "Those who are well have no need of a physician, but those who are sick. Go and learn what this means, 'I desire mercy, and not sacrifice.' For I came not to call the righteous, but sinners."

PEOPLE: Glory to you, O Lord, glory to you.

Then the deacon recites the litany:

Litany

DEACON: Have mercy on us, O God, in your great loving-kindness: we pray you, hear us, and have mercy.

PEOPLE: Lord, have mercy. (3)

DEACON: Again we pray for mercy, life, peace, health, salvation, and remission of sins of the servant of God (name).

PEOPLE: Lord, have mercy. (3)

DEACON: That he(she) may be pardoned every transgression, let us pray to the Lord.

PEOPLE: Lord, have mercy. (3)

PRIEST: For you are a merciful God who loves mankind, and to you we give glory, to the Father, and to the Son, and to the Holy Spirit, now and ever, and unto ages of ages.

PEOPLE: Amen.

Prayer

DEACON: Let us pray to the Lord.

PEOPLE: Lord, have mercy.

SEVENTH PRIEST: O Master, Lord our God, Physician of souls and bodies, you cure chronic illnesses and heal every disease and every infirmity among the people; you desire that all should be saved and come to the knowledge of the truth; you desire not the death of the sinner, but that he should repent and live. For you, O Lord, in the old covenant appointed repentance for sinners, for David and the Ninevites, and for those who went before them. Likewise, in the dispensation of your coming in the flesh, you called not the righteous but sinners to repentance; you accepted the repentance of the publican, the harlot, the thief, and of Paul, the great blasphemer and persecutor; you accepted the repentance of Peter, your first apostle, who thrice denied you, and you declared to him: "You are Peter, and on this rock I will build my church, and the gates of Hades shall not prevail against it. I will give you the keys of the kingdom of heaven." Because of your faithful promise, O good One who loves mankind, we too have boldness, and at this hour we pray you and ask: Hear our prayer, receive it as incense offered before you; visit your servant (name). If he(she) has sinned in word, or deed, or thought, at night or by day; if he(she) has been excommunicated by a priest, or come under anathema; if he(she) has been embittered by an oath or cursed himself(herself)—we pray and entreat you: Loose, pardon, and forgive him(her), O God, overlooking his(her) sins and transgressions, committed both knowingly and unknowingly. If he(she) has transgressed your commandments, or has sinned because he(she) bears flesh and dwells in the world, or through the wiles of the devil, forgive him(her), for you are a good God and you love mankind; for there is no man who lives and does not sin. You alone are sinless, and your righteousness endures for ever, and your word is truth. You have created humanity not for perdition, but for the keeping of your commandments and the inheritance of eternal life. And to you we give glory, together with the Father and the Holy Spirit, now and ever, and unto ages of ages.

PEOPLE: Amen.

Having completed this prayer, the seventh priest anoints the sick person with oil, reciting the following prayer:

Prayer of Anointing

O holy Father, Physician of souls and bodies, who sent your only-begotten Son, our Lord Jesus Christ, who heals every infirmity and delivers from death: heal also your servant (name) from the infirmities of body and soul which afflict him(her), and enliven him(her) with the grace of your Christ; through the prayers of our most-holy Lady, the Theotokos and ever-virgin Mary; through the intercessions of the honorable, bodiless powers of heaven; through the power of the precious and life-giving cross; through the protection of the honorable, glorious prophet, forerunner, and baptist, John; of the holy, glorious, and most-blessed apostles; of the holy, glorious, victorious martyrs; of our venerable and God-bearing fathers; of the holy unmercenary physicians, Cosmas and Damian, Cyrus and John, Panteleimon and Hermolaus, Sampson and Diomedes, Photius and Anicetas; of the holy and righteous ancestors of God, Joachim and Anna; and of all the saints. For you are the fountain of healing, O our God, and to you we give glory, to the Father, and the Son, and the Holy Spirit, now and ever, and unto ages of ages. Amen.

Prayer of Absolution

After the anointing, the clergy gather around the sick person. The first priest takes the gospel book, opens it, and places it, with the writing down, on the head of the sick person, with all the priests holding the book. The first priest, who does not place his hand on the gospel, recites the following prayer:

O holy King, compassionate and of great mercy, Lord Jesus Christ, Son and Word of the living God, you desire not the death of a sinner, but that he should repent and live: it is not my sinful hand that I lay upon the head of him(her) who approaches you in sin and asks, through us, for the forgiveness of his(her) sins; but it is your strong and mighty hand, which is in this, your holy gospel, held by my fellow-ministers over the head of your servant (name). With them, I also pray and entreat your merciful love for humanity, which remembers not evil, O God our Savior, who through your prophet Nathan granted forgiveness of sins to the penitent David, and who accepted Manasses' prayer of repentance: in your customary love for humanity, accept also this your servant (name), who repents of his(her) own sins, and overlook his(her) transgressions. For you are our God, who commanded us to forgive those who fall into sin, even unto seventy times seven. For as is your majesty, so also is your mercy, and to you belong all glory, honor, and worship, now and ever, and unto ages of ages. Amen.

They remove the gospel book from the head of the sick person and present it to him(her) to kiss.

Then the deacon recites the litany:

Litany

DEACON: Have mercy on us, O God, in your great loving-kindness: we pray you, hear us, and have mercy.

PEOPLE: Lord, have mercy. (3)

DEACON: Again we pray for mercy, life, peace, health, salvation, and remission of sins of the servant of God (name).

PEOPLE: Lord, have mercy. (3)

DEACON: That he(she) may be pardoned every transgression, let us pray to the Lord.

PEOPLE: Lord, have mercy. (3)

PRIEST: For you are a merciful God who loves mankind, and to you we give glory, to the Father, and to the Son, and to the Holy Spirit, now and ever, and unto ages of ages.

PEOPLE: Amen.

Troparia

The choir sings the following troparia, in tone 4.

Glory . . .

You have a fountain of healing, O holy unmercenaries; you grant healing to all who ask, for you have been accounted worthy of very great gifts by our Savior, the ever-flowing source. For the Lord has said to you, whose zeal equals that of the apostles: Behold, I have given you power over the unclean spirits, to cast them out, and to heal every sickness and every infirmity. For nobly you have lived, according to his commandments; freely you have received, freely give, healing the diseases of our souls and bodies.

Now and ever . . .

Theotokion: Regard the prayers of your servants, O all-pure One, for you stem the fierce attacks upon us and release us from all afflictions. You alone do we have as our anchor sure and strong, and we are under your protection. When we call on you, O Lady, we shall not be put to shame. Make haste to the petitions of those who cry to you in faith: Hail, O Lady, help of all, the joy, refuge, and salvation of our souls!

Dismissal

CHOIR: Glory to the Father, and to the Son, and to the Holy Spirit, now and ever, and unto ages of ages. Amen.

Lord, have mercy. (3) Father bless.

PRIEST: May Christ our true God, through the prayers of his most-pure Mother, through the power of the precious and life-giving cross, of the holy, glorious, praiseworthy Apostle James, the first bishop of Jerusalem and brother of God, and of all the saints, save us and have mercy on us, for he is good and loves humanity.

And the person who has received anointing bows, saying:

Bless me, holy fathers, and pardon me, a sinner. (3)

And having received their blessing and pardon, he(she) goes out, giving thanks to God.

An Abbreviated
Rite of Anointing[1]

A small table is prepared, and on it is placed a bowl of wheat and a gospel book. An empty vigil lamp is set on the wheat, and a cotton swab for anointing is placed in the wheat surrounding the lamp. Two containers, one with olive oil, the other with water (or red wine), are also placed next to it. The presbyter stands before the table, vested in his epitrachilion and phelonion and holding a candle. The priest incenses three times around the table, then the entire church or house, and the people. Then he stands before the table, facing east, and begins, saying:

PRIEST: Blessed is our God, always, now and ever, and unto ages of ages.

READER: Amen. Holy God, Holy Mighty, Holy Immortal, have mercy on us. (3) Glory to the Father, and to the Son, and to the Holy Spirit, now and ever and unto ages of ages. Amen. O most holy Trinity, have mercy on us. Lord, cleanse us from our sins.

[1]This abbreviated rite is intended for emergency use in a hospital or at home. It is based on a typical adaptation found in a 14th–15th-century Slavic manuscript (*Moscow Theological Academy no. 85*, ff 242–49), described by A. Golubtsov, "Ob obriadovoi storone tainstva eleosviashcheniia," 118.

Master, pardon our transgressions. Holy One, visit and heal our infirmities for your name's sake.

Lord, have mercy. (3)

Our Father, who art in heaven, hallowed be thy name. Thy kingdom come. Thy will be done, on earth as it is in heaven. Give us this day our daily bread; and forgive us our trespasses, as we forgive those who trespass against us; and lead us not into temptation, but deliver us from evil.

PRIEST: For yours is the kingdom, and the power, and the glory of the Father, and of the Son, and of the Holy Spirit, now and ever, and unto ages of ages.

Then the troparia are sung:

Have mercy on us, O Lord, have mercy on us. For we sinners, void of all defense, offer to you, as to our Master, this petition: Have mercy on us.

Glory . . .

Have mercy on us, O Lord, for in you have we trusted, and do not be very angry with us, nor remember our iniquities. But look down even now on us, for you are of tender compassion, and deliver us from our enemies. For you are our God, and we are your people. We are all the work of your hand, and we call on your name.

Now and ever . . .

Open to us the door of your loving-kindness, O blessed Theotokos. Because we have set our hope on you, may we not fail, but through you may we be delivered from all adversities: for you are the salvation of all Christians.

Then the deacon, or the principal priest, recites the following litany:

Litany

DEACON: In peace, let us pray to the Lord.

PEOPLE: Lord, have mercy.

DEACON: For the peace from above, and for the salvation of our souls, let us pray to the Lord.

PEOPLE: Lord, have mercy.

DEACON: For this holy house, and for those who enter it with faith, reverence, and the fear of God, let us pray to the Lord.

PEOPLE: Lord, have mercy.

DEACON: That he will bless this oil through the power, operation, and descent of the Holy Spirit, let us pray to the Lord.

PEOPLE: Lord, have mercy.

DEACON: For the servant of God (name), that God may visit him(her), and that the grace of the Holy Spirit may come upon him(her), let us pray to the Lord.

PEOPLE: Lord, have mercy.

DEACON: That he will deliver him(her) and us from all affliction, wrath, danger, and distress, let us pray to the Lord.

PEOPLE: Lord, have mercy.

DEACON: Help us, save us, have mercy on us, and protect us, O God, by your grace.

PEOPLE: Lord, have mercy.

DEACON: Remembering our most holy, pure, most blessed and glorious Lady, the Theotokos and ever-virgin Mary, with all the saints, let us commit ourselves, and one another, and our whole life to Christ our God.

PEOPLE: To you, O Lord.

Then the priest recites the "Prayer of the Oil" over the vigil lamp, into which he pours some oil.

Prayer of the Oil

O Lord, in your mercy and compassion, you heal the afflictions of our souls and bodies: sanctify now this oil, O Master, that it may bring healing to those who are anointed with it, relief from every passion, from every sickness of flesh and spirit, and from all evil; and so that your holy name may be glorified, of the Father, and of the Son, and of the Holy Spirit, now and ever, and unto ages of ages.

PEOPLE: Amen.

Prokeimenon

DEACON: Let us be attentive.

FIRST PRIEST: Peace be to all.

READER: And to your spirit.

DEACON: Wisdom.

READER: The Prokeimenon in the first tone. Let your steadfast love, O Lord, be upon us, even as we hope on you. (Ps 33[32].22)

verse: Rejoice in the Lord, O you righteous! Praise befits the upright. (Ps 33[32].1)

Epistle (James 5.10–16)

DEACON: Wisdom.

READER: The reading is from the General Epistle of St James.

DEACON: Let us be attentive.

READER: Brethren, as an example of suffering and patience, take the prophets who spoke in the name of the Lord. Behold, we call those happy who were steadfast. You have heard of the steadfastness of Job, and you have seen the purpose of the Lord, how the Lord is compassionate and merciful. But above all, my brethren, do not swear, either by heaven or by earth or with any other oath, but let your yes be yes and your no be no, that you may not fall under condemnation. Is any one among you suffering? Let him pray. Is any cheerful? Let him sing praise. Is any among you sick? Let him call for the elders of the church, and let them pray over him, anointing him with oil in the name of the Lord; and the prayer of faith will save the sick man, and the Lord will raise him up; and if he has committed sins, he will be forgiven. Therefore confess your sins to one another, and pray for one another, that you may be healed. The prayer of a righteous man has great power in its effects.

PRIEST: Peace be to you.

179

READER: And to your spirit. Alleluia, alleluia, alleluia. *(tone 8)*

PEOPLE: Alleluia, alleluia, alleluia.

READER, *verse:* I will sing of loyalty and of justice; to you, O Lord, I will sing. (Ps 101[100].1)

PEOPLE: Alleluia, alleluia, alleluia.

Gospel (John 5.2–24)

DEACON: Wisdom. Attend. Let us listen to the Holy Gospel.

PRIEST: Peace be to all.

PEOPLE: And to your spirit.

PRIEST: The reading is from the Holy Gospel according to Saint John.

PEOPLE: Glory to you, O Lord, glory to you.

DEACON: Let us be attentive.

PRIEST: Now there is in Jerusalem by the Sheep Gate a pool, in Hebrew called Bethesda, which has five porticoes. In these lay a multitude of invalids, blind, lame, paralyzed. One man was there, who had been ill for thirty-eight years. When Jesus saw him and knew that he had been lying there a long time, he said to him, "Do you want to be healed?" The sick man answered him, "Sir, I have no man to put me into the pool when the water is troubled, and while I am going another steps down before me." Jesus said to him, "Rise, take up your pallet, and walk." And at once the man was healed, and he took up his pallet and walked.

Now that day was the Sabbath. So the Jews said to the man who was cured, "It is the Sabbath, it is not lawful for you to carry your pallet." But he answered them, "The man who healed me said to me, 'Take up your pallet, and walk.' " They asked him, "Who is the man who said to you, 'Take up your pallet, and walk'?" Now the man who had been healed did not know who it was, for Jesus had withdrawn, as there was a crowd in the place. Afterward, Jesus found him in the temple, and said to him, "See, you are well! Sin no more, that nothing worse befall you." The man went away and told the Jews that it was Jesus who had healed him. And this was why the Jews persecuted Jesus, because he did this on the Sabbath. But Jesus answered them, "My Father is working still, and I am working." This was why the Jews sought all the more to kill him, because he not only broke the Sabbath but also called God his Father, making himself equal with God.

Jesus said to them, "Truly, truly, I say to you, the Son can do nothing of his own accord, but only what he sees the Father doing; for whatever he does, that the Son does likewise. For the Father loves the Son, and shows him all that he himself is doing; and greater works than these will he show him, that you may marvel. For as the Father raises the dead and gives them life, so also the Son gives life to whom he will. The Father judges no one, but has given all judgment to the Son, that all may honor the Son, even as they honor the Father. He who does not honor the Son does not honor the Father who sent him. Truly truly, I say to you, he who hears my word and believes him who sent me, has eternal life; he does not come into judgment, but has passed from death to life."

PEOPLE: Glory to you, O Lord, glory to you.

Prayer of Anointing

O holy Father, Physician of souls and bodies, who sent your only-begotten Son, our Lord Jesus Christ, who heals every infirmity and delivers from death: heal also your servant (name) from the infirmities of body and soul which afflict him(her), and enliven him(her) with the grace of your Christ; through the prayers of our most-holy Lady, the Theotokos and ever-virgin Mary; through the intercessions of the honorable, bodiless powers of heaven; through the power of the precious and life-giving cross; through the protection of the honorable, glorious prophet, forerunner, and baptist, John; of the holy, glorious, and most-blessed apostles; of the holy, glorious, victorious martyrs; of our venerable and God-bearing fathers; of the holy unmercenary physicians, Cosmas and Damian, Cyrus and John, Panteleimon and Hermolaus, Sampson and Diomedes, Photius and Anicetas; of the holy and righteous ancestors of God, Joachim and Anna; and of all the saints. For you are the fountain of healing, O our God, and to you we give glory, to the Father, and the Son, and the Holy Spirit, now and ever, and unto ages of ages. Amen.

After the prayer, the priest takes one of the cotton swabs, dips it into the holy oil, and anoints the sick person, crosswise, on the brows, the nostrils, the cheeks, the lips, the breast, and on both sides of the hands. As he anoints the sick person, he recites the following prayer:

O good God who loves mankind, compassionate and greatly merciful, abundant in mercy and rich in goodness, Father of mercies and God of all consolation, who through the apostles has given us power to heal the infirmities of your people through oil and prayer: make this oil to be for the healing of those who are anointed with it, for relief from every disease and all sickness, for deliverance from evil of those who in hope await salvation from you. Yea, O Master, Lord, our God almighty, we entreat you to save us all. O only Physician of our souls and bodies, sanctify us all. You heal every disease; heal also your servant (name): raise him(her) up from the bed of sickness, through the mercies of your kindness; visit him(her) with your mercy and compassion; remove from him(her) every illness and infirmity; so that, having been raised up by your mighty hand, he(she) may serve you with all thanksgiving; and that we too, who now share in your ineffable love for humanity, may hymn and glorify you, for you perform great and wondrous deeds, extraordinary and glorious. For you are merciful and save us, O God, our God, and to you we give glory, together with your only-begotten Son and your all-holy, good, and life-giving Spirit: now and ever, and unto ages of ages.

PEOPLE: Amen.

Then the deacon recites the litany:

Litany

DEACON: Have mercy on us, O God, in your great loving-kindness: we pray you, hear us, and have mercy.

PEOPLE: Lord, have mercy. (3)

DEACON: Again we pray for mercy, life, peace, health, salvation, and remission of sins of the servant of God [name].

PEOPLE: Lord, have mercy. (3)

DEACON: That he(she) may be pardoned every transgression, let us pray to the Lord.

PEOPLE: Lord, have mercy. (3)

PRIEST: For you are a merciful God who loves mankind, and to you we give glory, to the Father, and to the Son, and to the Holy Spirit, now and ever, and unto ages of ages.

PEOPLE: Amen.

Dismissal

PEOPLE: Glory to the Father, and to the Son, and to the Holy Spirit, now and ever, and unto ages of ages. Amen.

Lord, have mercy. (3) Father bless.

PRIEST: May Christ our true God, through the prayers of his most-pure Mother, through the power of the precious and life-giving cross, of the holy, glorious, praiseworthy Apostle James, the first bishop of Jerusalem and brother of God, and of all the saints, save us and have mercy on us, for he is good and loves mankind.

PEOPLE: Amen.

Suggestions for Further Reading

Cabasilas, Nicholas. *The Life in Christ*. Translated by Carmino J. deCatanzaro. Crestwood, NY: SVS Press, 1974.

Constantelos, Demetrios J. "The Interface of Medicine and Religion in the Greek and the Christian Greek Orthodox Tradition." *Greek Orthodox Theological Review* 33 (1988): 1–17.

Glen, Jennifer M. "Sickness and Symbol: The Promise of the Future." *Worship* 54 (1980): 397–411.

Gusmer, Charles W. *And You Visited Me: Sacramental Ministry to the Sick and the Dying*. Rev. ed. New York: Pueblo, 1989.

Harakas, Stanley S. *Health and Medicine in the Eastern Orthodox Tradition*. New York: Crossroad, 1990.

––––––. "'Rational Medicine' in the Orthodox Tradition." *Greek Orthodox Theological Review* 33(1988): 19–43.

Hutcheon, Cyprian Robert. "The *Euchelaion*—Mystery of restoration: Anointing in the Byzantine Tradition." *Worship* 76 (2002): 25–42.

Kasza, John C. *Understanding Sacramental Healing: Anointing and Viaticum*. Chicago: Hillenbrand Books, 2006.

Meyendorff, Paul. "The Anointing of the Sick: Some Pastoral Considerations." *St Vladimir's Theological Quarterly* 35 (1991): 241–55.

O'Connell, Matthew J., trans. *Temple of the Holy Spirit: Sickness and Death of the Christian in the Liturgy.* New York: Pueblo, 1983. A collection of articles, many by Orthodox authors.

Schmemann, Alexander. *For the Life of the World: Sacraments and Orthodoxy.* 2d ed. Crestwood, NY: SVS Press, 1973.

Talley, Thomas. "Healing: Sacrament or Charism?" *Worship* 46 (1972): 518–527.

Zizioulas, John D. *Being as Communion: Studies in Personhood and the Church.* Crestwood, NY: SVS Press, 1985.